The Way

to

Will-Power

BY
Henry Hazlitt

"The strength of your life is measured by the strength of your will."—Henry Van Dyke

Owlfoot Press
2016

*Copyright © Owlfoot Press, Rawtenstall, 2016.
First published by E.P. Dutton, New York, 1922.*

CONTENTS

Chapter		Page
I	A Revelation	1
II	The Intellect as a Valet	5
III	The Price One Pays	13
IV	Old Bottles for the New Wine	17
V	Resolutions Made and Resolutions Kept	25
VI	Success and the Capital S	31
VII	The Scale of Values	35
VIII	Controlling One's Thoughts	41
IX	The Omnipresence of Habit	47
X	The Alteration of Habit	55
XI	Will and the Psychoanalysts	63
XII	Concentration	79
XIII	A Program of Work	87
XIV	The Daily Challenge	93
XV	Second and Third Winds	99
XVI	Moral Courage	111

I
A REVELATION

YOU have seen the advertisements. The lion and the man are facing each other; the man upstanding, hands clenched, his look defiant and terrible; the lion crouching. Who will win? The man, without doubt. He has what the beast lacks, Will-Power.

And at the bottom of the page is the triangular clipping which you cut out and send for the book on how to acquire it.

Or perhaps the advertisement promises you a $10,000 a year position. Nothing less than $10,000 a year seems capable of attracting the present-day reader of twenty-cent magazines. And those positions, one learns, are reserved for the men of Will-Power (not forgetting the capitals).

The advertisements betray bizarre ideas about the will and will-power. Any one who has the remotest notion of psychology might be led from them to suspect the advertised course. But the advertisements reflect not alone the advertiser's ideas, but the ideas of the plain man. They are written to catch the plain man's eye, and they do catch his eye, how else to account for their persistence, their enlargement and their multiplication, notwithstanding the notorious expensiveness of advertising?

Now I am about to reveal a profound secret about the will. The revelation will cause a good deal of shock and disappointment and a bedlam of protest. However, I derive courage to meet the protest because I have an imposing body of psychologic opinion behind me. I have behind me most of the reputable psychologic opinion since Herbert Spencer. And so here it is:

The will does not exist.

I repeat it, lest you fancy there has been a misprint. There is no such thing as the will. Nor such a thing as will-power. These are merely convenient words.

Now when a man denies the existence of the will he is on dangerous ground. It is as if he were to deny the existence of the tomato. Yet I do deny that the will exists, in anything like the same sense that the tomato exists. The tomato is a definite entity. You can pick it up, handle it, feel it, or throw it at the person who denies its existence. And this evidence of reality may convince him. But I am not so crude nor so fatuous as to deny the existence of the will simply because you cannot feel it or taste it. I do not deny it simply because it is not material and tangible. I deny it because it is not even spiritual. The plain man's conception of the will is utterly and grotesquely wrong, and he must be shaken from it violently.

The popular conception seems to be that the Creator, having decided that a man might want to have a brain to use upon occasion, bethought Himself about the ingredients, and dropped in first a memory, then an imagination, then a will, and then a power to reason. Though popular conception is vague on the details, it is probably that the last was a small parcel, wrapped in prejudices to protect it from strain.

But the Creator could have left out the will, and no one would have been the wiser. Proof of it is that so few of us were. It was only recently that psychologists began to suspect its absence.

You are making a gesture of impatience. "This is a little to stiff," you say. "There is a limit to which you can impose on me. I know when a man shows a will, and when he doesn't. I have met strong-willed men, and I have met weak-willed men, and I know the difference when I see it."

For your remonstrance I have the greatest respect. And I will now proceed to give heed to it.

II
THE INTELLECT AS A VALET

HAVING given some hint of what the will is not, it is now my pleasant duty to tell what it is. This may best be done by illustration.

You resolve to abolish late nights. Two nights out a week will be your limit. No night out later than midnight. It doesn't pay. A man loses sleep. He hurts his health. He isn't as fresh as he ought to be for work. He is just frittering his time away, and getting nowhere, and not improving himself evenings, and it's expensive,—

So you resolve to cut it out. With a free conscience you make your two engagements for the coming week. About Monday noon Jones drops around at the office. There is a little game of poker toward some night that week when they can get the crowd together. Now poker is marvelously fascinating. You haven't seen the boys for a long time. And you hate to lie to Jones, and tell him all your nights are occupied, for such a little reason. And you are ashamed to tell him the truth. That you have resolved to go out only two nights a week, come what may, might strike Jones as deliciously funny. He might tell the boys, who also have a sense of humor. And there is the possibility that Jones might be offended. So you look straight before you, undecided for a minute or two, or you make feeble excuses (not your real ones) which are easily overridden by Jones, and you end by thinking to yourself that you will not count this week, or that you will make up for it the week after.... And your dishonor is complete.

Let us analyze this degrading incident. Man is a bundle of desires. He desires this, and that, and something else again. And the world is so constituted that, in nearly every instance, one desire cannot be attained save at the sacrifice of some other. This provoking state of affairs was long ago crystallized in the phrase that you cannot eat your cake and have it too. More broadly, it may be expressed in the phrase that everything we desire has its price. The price of a cake is a dollar; the price of keeping your dollar is the loss of a cake.

This illuminating truth does not stop at the grossly material things, at the things whose prices can be measured in money. It extends throughout the spiritual universe. The price of earning $2 extra a day may be working an extra hour a day; which may be conceived either as a pain of extra hour's work or as the loss of an hour's leisure. Conversely, the price of an hour's extra leisure a day is $2 a day.

We are now coming to grips with our actual case. The price of staying out late at night is sleep, health, efficiency at business, money, and self-improvement. That is, these are the things that the man must pay, lose, sacrifice, in order that he may stay out late at night. Conversely, the price of sleep, health, efficiency at business, money, self-improvement, is the pleasure of staying out late at night that one gives up.

We have taken a devious course to arrive at our conclusion, yet we must deviate a little further before we come back. We must consider the Intellect. For centuries we have glorified the intellect; we have put wreaths upon its head and sung its praises. Which is quite absurd. For a man's intellect is a helpless, powerless sort of thing, a mere instrument, a tool, a subordinate, which the desires boss around. It does the bidding of the desire that shouts the loudest. You my call this a libel on the intellect. You perhaps maintain the traditional view that the intellect directs the desires.

But reflect. You engage daily in more or less unpleasant tasks for eight hours; you work. It is your desire for bread and soup and café parfait, for an overcoat, an apartment, and theatres and golf, that drives you there. You may protest that you enjoy your work. I shall not gainsay you. In either case, it is your desires that are dictating your action. The intellect merely obeys. If it is a good intellect, its owner may count himself fortunate. It will be better able to carry out the orders of its bosses, the desires; it will satisfy them more, and it will satisfy more of them. The intellect may, and often does, pick the road to a given place; the desires always dictate the designation. To multiply figures, the intellect is the steering gear, the desires are the engine; the intellect is the pilot, the desires are the breeze.

We are now ready to return to our immediate subject. When a man is engaged in what we call making a decision, the intellect may be thought to occupy a place of greater dignity. It may be imaged as acting as a judge between conflicting desires. But the position of the intellect is in reality one of profound humiliation. In deciding between desires, it is actually trying to make up its mind which desire is the stronger. It feels their muscles, so to speak. And it obeys the desire with the hardest biceps.

Now every decision is not merely a selection from among desires. One desire may be so overpowering that all others cringe before it; they are merely brushed out of the way. The function of the intellect, then, in making a decision, is to select from alternative courses the one which most promises to fulfill this supreme desire.

I can fancy your rebelling at this point, if in fact, you have not done so long ago. "What you say may be all very true about some people," I can hear you saying, "but suppose I refuse to allow my intellect to be bullied around in this shameless manner? Suppose I choose to have my intellect snap its fingers at all my desires, and say 'Hereafter *I* will be master?' What becomes of all your fine analysis then?"

This question, my dear sir, is not so formidable as it looks. What it would amount to, if you succeeded in carrying out your magnificent defiance, or rather, if you succeeded in thinking you had, would be that your desire (note the word), your desire to have your intellect master would overcome other desires or impulses, recognized by your intellect as such, which arose transiently from moment to moment. You would act only on the desires which your intellect happened to approve of; but that is merely another way of saying that your desire to act on the principles of common sense had overcome all other desires.

For mark. There is nothing immoral in desires *per se*. There are good desires as well as evil. There are spiritual desires as well as material. There are desires to help others, to spread cheerfulness, to protect one's health, to live in moderation, to feel satisfied with one's lot, to "succeed" in life, to go to Heaven, to feel the happiness that virtue gives. And these desires may be just as powerful as selfish desires, or as a craving for transient sensual pleasures. Bernard Shaw says somewhere that real goodness is nothing but the self-indulgence of a good man.

Unfortunately, the word "desire" taken by itself, has come into popular usage to have a restricted, a sensual, an evil meaning. Popular usage has perverted it just as it has perverted the word "pleasure," which arouses such endless confusion of thought in ethical argument. I verily believe that could a man be brought to think of the word "desire" always in its true and broadest meaning, his aversion to the truth that the desires over-lord the intellect would be completely removed.

For as a fact, I have greatly understated the predominance of the desires as compared with the intellect. The very existence of the intellect depends upon the desires. Unless a man have desires, he will have no intellect. Or rather, he will never develop it and never use it, which is much the same thing. Thinking is problem solving. It arises from thwarted purposes. If we have no desires, we can have no purposes, and hence nothing to thwart. Thinking may arise as an attempt to solve something bearing on our immediate personal welfare, or on the welfare of our family or our city, or on the welfare of mankind; it may arise from the love of prestige and applause or from sheer intellectual curiosity. In any case, desire of some kind is the motivating force.

A great difficulty yet remains. You may admit that the intellect is a servant and not a master. But not that it is the servant of your desires. "It is the servant of Me," you say. "It is the servant of My Will." These are two distinct perhaps contradictory, assertions. Let us consider the first.

Now let me ask. What are you? You are nothing but a total. Take away your body, take away your physical brain, take away your intellect, your desires, your memory, your imagination, take away, I say, all the parts and attributes of you, and there is nothing left. That should be obvious, so obvious that I almost blush to state it. Whenever you speak of Me, or I, or You, you are speaking now of one part or attribute of yourself, now of another. You say, "I intend to do so-and-so"—meaning that a certain desire within you is going to make the rest of you do so-and-so. You say, "I am running,"—meaning that your legs are running, carrying the rest of your body and your brain along with them. You say, "I am thinking,"—meaning that your intellect is thinking. Your knees aren't thinking; your feet aren't thinking; your teeth aren't thinking. Only your intellect. In any case, when you refer to *I*, you are referring now to one part of yourself, now to another; now to another; and yet, such is the confusion of thought, that because you give the same name now to one part and now to another, you fancy that the word "I" refers to something distinct from any of these, something in addition, something separable from the parts that compose it.

But when you are talking of *"I,"* in the foregoing sense, you are usually referring to your Will, and it is this conception that we must now consider. The brain, as previously intimated, is a receptacle full of conflicting desires. (All desires are not ever-present, but that is not a point we need consider now.) For certain periods—it may be only for a moment, perhaps for a day, possibly for half a lifetime—a certain desire will predominate. That desire, for just as long as it predominates, will determine action. For as long as it predominates and determines action, that desire constitutes your will. It is what you desire to do, what you want to do, what you *will* to do.

But one desire may predominate for one hour, and another the next. Just now you may wish to sit home for the evening and improve your mind. That is your will. After reading this a few minutes you may become bored (I am not blaming you), and may decide to call up your friends and play bridge for the evening. That is also your will.

And here we come to the great confusion. These desires, which are constantly gaining individual supremacy and losing it, which are constantly overthrowing and dethroning each other like presidents in a South American republic, are each of them mere temporary holders of power. Yet we give a permanent name to them. We call one desire the will, and we call the next desire the will. And so we think that the will is something in addition to these separate desires. If we were to say that Warren G. Harding kissed Mrs. Harding, and then were to add that the President of the United States also kissed Mrs. Harding, the confusion between words and things would be obvious. The President of the Unite States we know to be only another name for Harding. It is merely a permanent name for the different temporary holders of that powerful office, all of different natures. So with the mind. The will is merely a name for the desire that happens to hold temporary power. Take away all desires, and there remains no will.

III
THE PRICE ONE PAYS

I can fancy that you are becoming somewhat weary. "What is the sense of this fellow's always harping on the same thing," you may say. "Here he has been going on for two chapters with his precious analysis, repeating himself, insisting, emphasizing, underestimating my intelligence, and after I have his point, and he has made himself clear, he keeps on talking. I picked up his book under the impression that it might help me to acquire more will-power, and here he is trying to jam a psychological treatise down my throat."

Now I admit the seeming justice of this. But my point is vital. Before we can acquire will-power, we must first of all know what we are talking about. An amazing amount of cant and nonsense is written about the will. I have seen a book on Will-Power so thick and for-midable that the chairs creaked when you put it upon them, and it was vitiated and full of absurdities from the first page to the last, simply because the author had not the remotest conception of what the will is. Occasionally there was a little sense, because occasionally the writer caught glimpses of the truth, as a man must in so many pages. But we cannot afford to catch only glimpses. We must know what we are talking about all the time, not merely in moments of absent-mindedness. My point, I repeat, is vital. I am taking no risks with it.

Having approached a true conception of the will, we are prepared to go a step farther, and to find what we mean by the phrase "Will-Power." This is not difficult. It resolves itself into a question of time. When we say a man has will-power, we mean that he has a certain desire which persists and predominates for a comparatively long period. It is not being constantly dethroned by a multitude of other desires. Either the other desires are not strong enough, or it is too strong for them (which as we shall see later, is more than a mere verbal distinction); and if perchance this desire is forced to abdicate for a little while, which may sometimes happen with the strongest-willed persons, it quickly throws out the usurping desire and reigns again.

This dominant desire is usually a wish for something remote. The man who obeys it is setting the expected advantage of the future against the supposed advantages of the present. He will not eat an extra slice of that delicious pie, for he knows that if he did he would two hours later be suffering the agonies of indigestion. He will not gaze at that pretty girl on the subway seat opposite, for he has embarked upon the noble enterprise of improving his mind; he has set aside his trip to work in the mornings for concentration on some serious subject; he will not be distracted. Or he will stay late at the office; he will take his work home with him; he will whip his brain on when it is tired; he will shorten his holidays, eliminate social enjoyments and endanger his health, for he has resolved upon Success in Life.

Will-Power, then, may be defined as the ability to keep a remote desire so vividly in mind that immediate desires which interfere with it are not gratified.

Understand me, I pass no moral judgment on the will *per se*. I do not condemn it, neither do I praise. It may be evil as well as good. A man may devote years to avenging himself upon another. He may put up with inconveniences; endure privation; submit to insults, humiliation, and risks of exposure, all of which he could avoid if he would consent to give up his aim. Napoleon consecrated his colossal will to the once glorious and now discredited occupation of trying to conquer the world.

But will does imply thought of the future. It is ready, if need be, to sacrifice the present to the future. And that is one of the great distinguishing marks between the civilized man and the savage. The savage did not save; he did not plant crops; he did not provide for old age. He did not even set aside food for the next day. When he got a piece of meat, he gorged himself, until he slept. He died young.

A firmer grasp of the true idea of will-power is attainable if one is acquainted with some of the distinctions of political economy. The economist differentiates between "desire" and "demand." When the layman talks of the demand for automobiles, he thinks usually of the desire for automobiles. The economist will not tolerate such looseness. A beggar may genuinely desire a Rolls Royce car, but that does not concern the manufacturer. It does not constitute part of the demand that the manufacturer must supply. He is interested only in the folk who can afford to pay for Rolls-Royce cars. And it is not only essential that the people who can afford a Rolls-Royce shall desire it, but *they must desire it so much that they are willing to pay the price for it.*

Now we are ready to apply this economic definition to the will. After thirteen pages of theory, exegesis and preparation, we are able to lay down the first rule for the aspirant for will-power. It is a very important rule, and, indeed, possibly covers most of the subject.

Before you make any formal resolutions whatsoever, make certain that you genuinely desire to carry it out. Let there be no doubt that the end you have in view is so desirable or advantageous that it will outweigh all desires and advantages or all other ends that are likely to have to be foregone or abandoned in order to attain it. In short, *be sure you are willing to pay the price.*

This rule is the corner-stone. Its importance will become more and more appreciated as we go on.

IV
OLD BOTTLES FOR THE NEW WINE

HAVING made myself satisfactorily clear, I am now disposed to become more amiable and conciliatory. Having demolished (I hope) popular misconceptions of the will and the intellect by gunpowder charges of the truth, and having erected a new edifice in place of the old, vague, and misleading one, I am willing to add a few bricks from the old building. In short, I am prepared to make concessions. It is probably quite wise and helpful to do this, because it causes less confusion and less irritation to talk, wherever possible, in terms of established conceptions than in terms of conceptions to which the reader is unaccustomed. This is all the more to be desired when the old conception has some partial justification, and when, though loosely lumping different things under one name, it none the less, by so doing, effects an economy of thought and of language.

I have said, for instance, that there is no such thing as the will considered as an entity, that it is simply a name we give first to one desire and then to another. But by way of setting off those desires which we commonly call "the will" from those desires which "the will" opposes, I have said that the will, in general, represents desires for remote, as opposed to immediate, gratifications. Yet we may generalize still further. As long as we keep in the background of our minds that the will is really an abstraction, there is no harm in speaking of it a good part of the time as if it were an entity; and insofar as it can be said to represent a definite and permanent entity, the will may be defined as *our desire to be a certain sort of character*. This is still a desire, you see, and it is still an abstraction; for our desire to be a certain sort of character may mean at one moment a desire to be honest, at another moment a desire not to get drunk, and at still another moment a desire to concentrate on something.

When we commonly speak of the will and think of it as if it were a definite concrete thing, it is this desire to be a certain sort of character, I think, that we commonly have in mind. When popular language says that a man is the slave of his desires, it means that he acts upon the cravings and impulses that from time to time arise, though in retrospect he will know that such actions would never be done by the kind of character he wants to be. When popular language says that a man is the master of his own desires, that he holds them in leash and under his control, it means that this *desire to be a certain kind of character* is at all times vivid and powerful enough to be acted upon in preference to any other fleeting or recurrent desire that may beckon him.

And it is, on the whole, rather well that popular language has this conception imbedded in it. For actions and decisions which would otherwise seem trivial are made by it to seem large and significant. It may not seem a matter of importance whether you take this particular drink or not, or whether you cheat the car-conductor out of this particular five-cent piece. But if you look upon the non-performance of this little act as your ability to refuse to yield to a particular impulse, and if your ability to refuse to yield to this particular impulse becomes in your mind *a challenge to and a test of your entire character*, you have thrown into the scale a mighty force to ensure your taking the right action.

If we accept the definition of will as the desire to be a certain kind of character, then it can be seen to be a matter of the highest importance just what kind of character you desire to be. A man may have a strong will but low ideals, or he may have high ideals and a weak will. A man ought to make two demands of his ideals; first that they be high enough, and second that they be his own.

If a man really and truly desires to be a roué or pickpocket, if this be his ideal, and if his conduct conforms absolutely with his principles, there is assuredly no fault to be found with his will. He may firmly put aside all distractions and conquer every good and noble temptation, in order to be a pickpocket or a roué. But society asks something more of him than strength of will. It asks that his ideals be socially beneficial. And even more may be required. It may be asked that a man put his ideals so high that it is difficult to reach them. As Browning has expressed it, "A man's reach should exceed his grasp, or what's a heaven for?" A man with lenient and unexacting ideals may be a tolerable character; he can never be a great one.

The demand that a man's ideals should be his own is one more difficult to comply with. It means he must not accept his moral canons and standards unquestioningly from the community. It means that he must not be afraid of "not doing what everybody else does" or of "doing what nobody else does." It means that he must not be a mere mimic or a sheep. He must think for himself. He must examine for himself the grounds of right and wrong, and not let the principles upon which his life is conducted be laid down for him merely by other people's opinions. He must not be afraid of criticism if he feels in his own heart that he is right. This is an exacting ideal. It requires the highest moral courage.

A man who lives up to this ideal may be a "dangerous" character. But we are not now discussing ethics, *per se*, but only will-power. He is the strong character, the great character. He may be a Tolstoy or a Nietzsche or a Eugene Debs; but he is a law unto himself. We may think his ethical ideas mistaken, and mistaken they may be; but we cannot but admire the strength of character which leads him to act them out in spite of social opposition. If the strength be sometimes misdirected, that is unfortunate; but the important thing, from our present standpoint, is whether it is there.

This reference to "the strong character," recalls a pronouncement by John Stuart Mill in his essay on Liberty. "It is not," he says, "because men's desires are strong that they act ill; it is because their consciences are weak."

This aphorism must first be analyzed in terms of our new conception of the will. A man's "conscience" is simply that group of desires to act socially, usefully, morally, conventionally, to secure the good opinion of his fellow men, or not to fall in his own estimation, not to offend or to give anger or sorrow to his God, or it may represent his desire to forward any other more ultimate end, to which the gratification of the immediate impulse or desire would be opposed.

If the belief that Mill is contradicting with his dictum is a half-truth, so, too, is his own statement. It is not the "conscience" in itself, nor the "evil" desires in themselves, that ultimately count; it is the relation of the one to the other. The stronger his desires, the stronger his conscience, or counter-desires, must be; the weaker his desires, the less need he has for a strong conscience.

But we usually, and rightly, regard the man with the stronger conscience as the stronger and more admirable character. We admire far more the man who has a violent craving for drink, but nevertheless fights it down, than we do the man who refrains from drinking, but has no great liking for it anyway. Their outward action may be the same, so far as its effect on themselves or society is concerned; but our untrained and unsophisticated judgments are right in attaching the importance they do to the inward struggle. For the weak man who refrains from drinking may not refrain from other actions just as personally or socially injurious that he has a greater desire for; whereas the man with the stronger conscience, who has been able to fight this desire in this case, may be depended upon to fight lesser desires more easily.

We all know the habit that many mothers have of holding up some little mollycoddle as a model to their boy: "You never see Clarence do that!" And we sympathize with the boy's contempt: "Ah, Him! He *couldn't* be bad!" A man who is good from docility, and not from stern self-control, has no character.

Mill recognizes this distinction, and in the passage following the sentence of his I have quoted, states powerfully the case for the man with stronger impulses:

> There is no natural connection between strong impulses and a weak conscience. The natural connection is the other way. To say that one person's desires and feelings are stronger and more various than those of another, is merely to say that he has more of the raw material of human nature, and is therefore capable, perhaps of more evil, but certainly of more good. Strong impulses are but another name for energy. Energy may be turned to bad uses; but more good may always be made of an energetic nature, than of an indolent and impassive one. Those who have most natural feeling, are always those who cultivated feelings may be made the strongest. The same strong susceptibilities which make the personal impulses vivid and powerful are also the source from whence are generated the most passionate love of virtue, and the sternest self-control.

I began this chapter with one concession to the older and more habitual way of looking at things, and I shall end it with another. The first had to do with the will, and this has to do with the intellect. I have said that the intellect is a mere valet to the desires, and I have made a good many other disparaging remarks about it. But I can fancy that you were left not only unconvinced, but angry. I can fancy someone's having said, while reading those remarks of mine: "My desires are determined by my intellect. A man's desires are not the desires of a rabbit. I desire to read Shakespeare and Schopenhauer; I actually prefer it to spending my evenings in a poolroom or with some pretty female thing. Has not my intellect formed my desires? Has not it dictated them? What sort of flapdoodle are you trying to tell me?"

Now before such an assault I am humble, and retreat with a magnanimous gesture. It is strictly true that the desires and the intellect cannot be separated. They interact. Our desires may originally determine the direction of our intellectual interests, but once our intellectual interests have taken a certain turn, they may awaken new desires, and abandon old ones. The reading of Nietzsche may change a man's ideals and aims in life. A desire for a life of study may suddenly turn into a desire for a life of "action."

We have defined will as the desire to become a certain sort of character. We have seen that, at critical moments, when the craving to do a certain thing threatens, like a great tidal wave, to sweep us helpless before it, it is this desire to become a certain sort of character which throws its weight in the scale with the other weaker desires to balance us; it is this desire which stands like a rock to cling to until the torrent has spent its force. It, too, may be swept away at times. But when it is, we know that it has not been strong enough. It is a warning that the breakwater has been too low and too weak. We must build it higher and stronger. We must strengthen this desire to become a certain sort of character.

The ideal that we actually form will depend upon our parents, our religion, our associates, our reading, our thinking, the traditions of the nation and the age in which we live. Many of these elements are intellectual, and to the extent that these determine our ideals, they determine part of our desires.

But even here we cannot say that the intellect *creates* our desires. Rather, it *transforms* them. They exist congenitally in the form of raw materials; or more strictly, they exist as a country's "natural resources" exist, waiting to be worked up by our environment and our intellect (itself shaped by environment) into the finished product. Practically all men are born with the sexual instinct. But though this particular instinct, in its raw state, may be present in equal degrees in three men, environment, training and intellect may so shape this raw material that the first man may elect to marry and lead a normal sexual life, the second may launch forth as a roué, and the third may enter and abide by the vows of the priesthood. Similarly, the pugnacious instinct, which makes dogs fight and men go to war, may also, through environment and the intellect, be discharged through the channels of football or a philosophical controversy. It is the same with gregariousness, or any other instinct. These are the materials; the desires the finished products.

But though the intellect can control the finished product, it cannot control the raw materials. One cannot lose an inborn instinct by thinking; one cannot create one by thinking. In this respect the intellect bears the same relations to the instincts as man bears to matter. He can transform it, beautify it, give it value, turn it to his purposes; but he cannot create it and he cannot destroy it.

And, if we are to consider this question in a truly philosophic, not to say a metaphysical manner, I may as well confess right here that in talking of "desires" and "the intellect" I have been doing a somewhat dubious thing. Perhaps the more philosophic view is that at times the whole man desires, and at times he thinks; but the one process is never entirely absent from the other. When I deal with this process, I deal with it rather crudely, making abstractions, treating abstractions as entities, hypostatizing them, making verbs into nouns. A man desires something, and I speak of "the desires"; he thinks something, and I speak of "the intellect." In doing this, I am merely following common usage; and, indeed, the conceptions imbedded in our very language practically compel me to adopt this usage if I am to prevent myself from becoming utterly obscure and transcendental. As this is supposed to be a practical manual, not a philosophic treatise, there will be no harm in continuing to talk in terms of these common conceptions. But I enter this qualification to ward off irrelevant attacks. I shall try to change the common conceptions of the nature and relations of "the will" and "the intellect" only insofar as I think it needful to change them for practical purposes.

And now, having presented my apologies and concessions, we can have done with this everlasting theorizing, and come to practical cases.

V
RESOLUTIONS MADE AND RESOLUTIONS KEPT

THE trouble with the average man is not that he neglects to make resolutions. The trouble is that he makes far too many resolutions. Making resolutions is sometimes his principal daily occupation. He is forever forgetting or breaking them, and that is why he has to make them all over again.

You, O reader, have probably been through this experience, so often that you dislike to be reminded of it. It is probably your consciousness of past events that has tempted you to read this book. Now there is something to be said for you. You realize your imperfections. You are splendidly dissatisfied with your present habits, your present mode of loving, your present station in life. You say to yourself, "This will never do." You see things as they would be if you could get up earlier in the morning, if you could break that absurd habit of setting your alarm clock for seven, getting up, shutting it off, going back to bed with the honest intention of taking just a five minutes' snooze, and not waking up until quarter to eight. Ridiculous as it is, the habit repeats itself morning after morning. You jump with a start; you have a wild notion that the alarm clock has played a trick on you; you dress in six minutes, shave in four, bolt your breakfast, make some excited, irritated, unkind remarks to your wife, start for the station or the street car like a man in a walking race, break into a run, curse the line waiting for tickets, and when you are finally aboard your train, which trudges along and loiters around stations as if all eternity were before it, you say to yourself, "This will never do."

In that ride on the train to your office, you see things as they might be. You see yourself getting up at seven, dressing at your leisure, eating breakfast in an expansive mood; no friction; no irritation; no squabbles with friend wife; no dreadful fear that you are going to miss your train, or that somebody will look first at you, at the clock, and then at you as you come in the office. In that ride on the train you have glimpsed perfection. And you make a tremendous resolution. "This thing has been going on long enough. It's preposterous. It has got to stop. Tomorrow I will get up at seven."

And what happens? Well, you arrive at the office and there are a number of things to occupy attention; your resolution, temporarily, drops out of mind. Jones (my chief illustrative standby) wanders in and suggests his little game of poker that night. It is conceivable that you are not ashamed to protest, and that you indicate your new desire to keep early hours. Jones assures you it won't be long; just a hand or two. You go. You arrive home at 1:30, having had, in the main, and evening not too stupid, but inwardly grumbling that you got back so late, or that somehow you couldn't have spent five hours at Jones's house and still have arrived home two hours after you left home. You go to bed; you sleep.... The alarm rings. Seven o'clock! You get up, automatically, in a daze, angry and resentful against the alarm that you yourself have set. You shut it off. You turn back toward the bed, like a marionette, without consciousness of a decision or of any thought whatever; you retrace your steps; you are about to get into bed again; a vague recollection of yesterday's resolution (and perhaps also it is the resolution of the day before yesterday and of the day before that) flits uneasily across your mind. But you are sleepy; sleep is indispensable; the trouble yesterday was not that you went back to bed, but that you overslept when you got there; Just a five minute snooze.... You awake.

Ten minutes to eight! Impossible! And in the midst of your five-minute dress, and your three-and-a-half minute shave, and your bolted breakfast, you still have a corner of your mind that is reflecting on what an ass you have been, and making a resolution that this must be stopped. And so on, as one day follows another.

The example is chosen at random. It is not an extreme example. It is not the most powerful I could have selected. But it suffices to illustrate my point. The trouble is that even in your moments on the train you never sufficiently convinced yourself that you really wanted to get up and stay up when the alarm rang. At nine o'clock in the morning, on your way to work, you have been thinking only of one side of the case; and at seven o'clock the next morning you have been thinking only of the other side.

Understand me, I am not saying that it would be to your advantage to make that resolve on the train. I do not contend that it would be better to get up at seven and take your time than to get up at quarter to eight and hurry. You are the judge of that. I disclaim any moral attitude whatever. But I insist that if you do make a resolve it should be carried out. There should be never an exception. This point is supreme. To make a resolve and break it is demoralizing. Though not a single other soul on earth should know it, though God himself should not know, you would know it. You would have to confess your failure to yourself. To break a resolve is to undermine your self-respect. To break a resolve is to lose faith in yourself. It shakes your confidence that you can keep any other. The next time you become suddenly disgusted with any action or habit, and you clench your teeth and your left fist, and are just about to drive your left fist into the open palm of your right, and say to yourself. "The next time I—"you are apt to stop short and think of your previous failure, and the bitter irony of it all may rush over you. You start at the very beginning with an unwholesome doubt of whether you are going to keep your resolve. And when self-respect and self-faith are gone, nothing else is worth while. But with every resolution kept, be it ever so small a resolution, your faith in your self grows. The keeping of the next resolution becomes tremendously easier. Will-power comes into its inheritance.

The moral of all this is that you should make fewer resolutions and keep more. The foolish resolution is the resolution made in a moment of passion and self-disgust. It is well that you should have such moments. It is of such moments that great achievements are born. But before you make a resolve that you seriously mean to execute, look at it coldly and completely. Think not alone of the benefits of keeping it, but of the disadvantages. If you have been lying in bed until quarter to eight, you have not been doing so unless there were some advantages to lying in bed until quarter to eight. Consider these advantages in the moment of your resolve. Do not pass them over in contempt. Weigh them at their full value. Measure the sacrifice of forsaking them. Balance it against the advantages of getting up promptly at seven. You may decide that getting up promptly at seven is not worth its price. You may decide to compromise on half past seven, which would allow you half an hour's more sleep and a little more time to dress. Upon what you decide it is not for me to comment. *But your decision should be carried out*. No more demoralizing course could be conceived than daily to resolve to arise at seven and the next day always to wait until a quarter to eight. Such a course comes only because, when you make your resolves, you do not fairly face the price.

This rule is so important, and has so wide a bearing, that we cannot forsake it here. It applies to all our resolves. Let me illustrate with the example that has become the favorite with all writers on will. I refer to drinking. The law-makers insist on solving this particular will-problem for us, but the Constitutional Amendment, so far as I am aware, puts no ban on its invaluable use as a literary example. Moreover, I cannot be arrested for pointing out that the actual temptations to drinking are not altogether a thing of the past.

You have a drink; then another. Perhaps you have one or two more, though the count becomes rather confusing after a time. The liquor "touches the spot," as you say, and for a time it produces a mental and emotional reaction that is highly delightful. But the next morning your stomach is upset; your food doesn't taste right; you have a headache; your mental and physical movements are slow and listless; you get little work done; the color of the universe is drab. You are probably minus a good deal of money. You feel your self-respect slipping. You are losing the respect of your friends. And your resolve that morning, accompanied with the usual terrible knitting of brow and clenching of fist and of teeth (as if that helped) is that these occasions of getting drenched must forever cease, end, terminate.

And then what? That acute psychologist, William James, can tell you much better than I:

> how many excuses does the drunkard find when each new temptation comes! It is a new brand of liquor which the interests of intellectual culture in such matters oblige him to test; moreover it is poured out and it is sin to waste it; also others are drinking and it would be churlishness to refuse. Or it is but to enable him to sleep or just to get through this job of work; or it isn't drinking, it is because he feels so cold; or it is Christmas-day; or it is a means of stimulating him to make a more powerful resolution in favor of abstinence than any he has hitherto made; or it is just this once, and one doesn't count, etc.,

etc., *ad libitum*—it is, in fact, anything you like except *being a drunkard. That* is the conception that will not stay before the poor soul's attention. But if he once gets able to pick out that way of conceiving form all the other possible ways of conceiving the various opportunities which occur, if through thick and thin he holds to it that this is being a drunkard and nothing else, he is not likely to remain one long. The effort by which he succeeds in keeping the right *name* unwaveringly present to his mind proves to be his saving moral act.

And how is he to get "able to pick out that way of conceiving" and hold to it? There is only one way. Not in the moment of temptation, but in the moment of his resolve, on "the morning after," that is the time for him to summon all these excuses before him, to bring up every possible excuse, to think of every conceivable advantage of drinking, and then to ask himself whether they are powerful enough to offset the conception of being a drunkard, or whether the advantages of drinking outweigh its disadvantages. He must give an honest answer then. If he ignores these excuses, on the ground that they are unworthy his noble resolve, he will find them dancing before his eyes in the next moment of temptation; and not having faced and answered them when he was in the mood to face and answer them, he is not likely to face them in that unhappy moment.

VI
SUCCESS AND THE CAPITAL S

I come now to a question, always thought of consequence, and growing year by year in the prominence assigned to it, until with some men it has become the sole pursuit in life. The present age is obsessed with its importance in a singular degree. The American nation is obsessed with it beyond all nations. Books are printed on it; magazines are devoted to it; men learnedly discuss its "secret." I refer, as the reader has probably divined, to the question of Success.

You observe that I spell it with the majuscule. The meaning of the word thus spelt is at once broader and narrower than that of the ordinary word. Broader, because it is taken to mean success in life. Narrower, because it has come to imply a peculiar kind of success. It means first of all a material success. It is a synonym for "getting on." Where you get to is thought of more consequence than what you are. Worshippers of Success hold in contempt the man who is capable of enjoying life in obscurity and on $30 a week. They measure happiness externally, not internally; objectively, not subjectively. Some (a growing clan) gauge success directly in proportion to the number of dollars on which a man pays income tax. Others, less narrow, would accord a place to fame, which is apparently conceived not so much as having the high estimation of one's fellows, as it is having one's name known among a large number of them.

Now implicitly or explicitly, this kind of extrinsic success is taken by the majority of persons as the measure of the intrinsic worth of a man. And that is why so many of us pursue it—not for itself, not because we personally would give a blackberry for it, not because it is indispensable to our inmost happiness, but simply that we may excite the envy of others and seem happy in their eyes. We have a strange habit of estimating our own happiness by what other persons think it is; and their opinion is likely to be based on our material success, since they have little else to go by. We continually try to obtain the things that the people around us want or profess to want, rather than what we want ourselves, because we have never really tried to examine whether there is any difference between the two. In trying to find whether we are hot or cold, we attach more importance to a dubious thermometer than we do to our own feelings.

Now this kind of success, which I have gone so far out of my way to become sarcastic about, is not commonly attainable without the possession for one characteristic, a characteristic of far more importance in this respect than thrift, intelligence, industry or common sense. That characteristic is a passionate *desire* to succeed, a desire so strong and overbearing that it amounts to a demand, and that, in the strictly economic sense to which I have before referred, means a *willingness to pay the price*.

The price is first of all singleness of purpose and concentration of effort. Nearly all of us, at school, have thought that we should some day like to be President of the Unite States. But not all of us have made it a point to study the lives of past presidents to see how they did it. Not all of us have taken a law course with that special end. Not all of us have refused tempting commercial opportunities for certain poverty and struggle for a time to gain an end in which the mathematical chances were ridiculously and overwhelmingly against us. Not all of us have kept desperately fanning the embers of dissatisfaction, fanning them into a constant white hot flame. With most of us the early fire dies; the embers fade and grow cool. We reach as high a level as we ever seriously hope to reach. We have spasms of dissatisfaction with our position in the world, but not sufficient dissatisfaction to make us work our way out of the rut to a higher position. We have moments of longing for the mountain tops, but not enough longing to make us willing to give up something for them. Strolling in the valleys is so much more pleasant than climbing.

And singleness of purpose demands more sacrifices than mere industry. It involves giving up all pleasures that interfere with it. They may be quite innocent pleasures, their sole offense being that they occupy time. It involves making oneself narrow; one cannot be a success in any one line if one dissipates one's energies in a number of activities—unless, of course, one be a versatile genius whose energies overflow, like Benjamin Franklin, Leonardo da Vinci, or Goethe—and such instances are so rare that they may be ignored.

Let there be no mistake. I do not mean to discourage efforts to become a Success. I mean merely to indicate that the goal has a price. I want you merely to ask yourself whether you are willing to pay that price; to ask yourself candidly how far you want to go and how much you are willing to pay; for if you do not ask yourself now, before you make your Success resolutions, you are likely to ask yourself later on. As you see obstacles and disappointments pile up, you are apt to begin wondering whether the game is worth the candle, whether the colors of the reality are as gorgeous as those of the painting. And if you decide to give up then, you will have broken your early resolution, with all the undermining of self-confidence and faith in your will which that involves.

VII
THE SCALE OF VALUES

IN spite of the disclaimer at the end of my last chapter, I am sure to be accused, because of the satiric remarks preceding that disclaimer, of disparaging Ambition, and I may not only be denounced for this, but I shall be told that of all places in which to disparage Ambition, a book purporting to show the way to will-power is the strangest and most unforgivable. But I hasten again to assure the reader that I have not disparaged Ambition at all; I have only disparaged ambitions. I have merely intimated that many of our ambitions are misdirected. We are worshipping false gods. A man in our day who laughs at the idea of taking seriously Zeus and Jupiter is not denounced as irreligious; in fact, he would probably be called irreligious if he did take them seriously. A time will come, I prophecy, when a man who bows down before our present popular conceptions of success will be denounced as lacking in ambition.

But there is a liability to misunderstanding more important that this. Many will derive the idea from some of my past remarks that the only thing I regard of importance is what a man actually does and does not want, and that I am not concerned with what he *ought* to want. This is a misinterpretation which cannot be allowed to pass. I have not and I cannot dwell at length upon what our ideals and aspirations ought to be; that is a subject for ethics, and I am talking of will-power. But for the sake of clarity, perhaps it were well that I indicate my position on this point.

We have seen that every ambition has its price, and that, before launching yourself formally upon the attainment of any ambition, you must first of all ask yourself whether it is worth its price. But the value of accomplishing an ambition, or the sacrifice involved in securing it, are not objective things. They exist in your own mind and they may be changed in your own mind.

An analogy may make this clearer. Whether or not you decide to pay $100 for an overcoat, depends both upon the value you attach to the overcoat and the value you attach to the $100. The worth you set upon the coat will depend upon whether you are without an overcoat altogether, or whether the one you have was acquired six years ago, or whether you just bought an overcoat last week. The value you attach to the overcoat will also depend upon whether you are enamored with the style of it, or whether you laugh at the style of it; and such things depend quite as much upon your own tastes as they do upon the overcoat. The value you attach to the $100 will depend upon your whole scale of values; your entire gamut of tastes and likes and dislikes; upon how many other uses you can think of for the $100, upon whether you attach more importance, say, to a $100 set of books; upon how much importance you attach to dress generally, and how much to money as a whole. In short, the value of a tangible object, unlike its weight, shape and dimensions, does not inhere in the object itself; it inheres in you. The weight of a long ton of coal will always be exactly the same as the weight of a long ton of bricks; but the value of a ton of coal will not always be $15, either to you or to the community as a whole.

Now what applies to economic values applies with equal force to social and moral values (and I am here speaking of these values as they are, not according to any notions of what they ought to be). These, too, exist not objectively, in the outward world, but in your own soul. When I advise you first to consider the price before setting out after any ambition, the decision you take may still differ from that of your neighbor who takes similar forethought. Imagine two men, each able to foresee perfectly all the consequences of his actions, and each trying to decide whether to make it his ambition to amass a million dollars. The first may enjoy putting forth effort; he may relish competition and strife; he may be satisfied with a narrow and exclusive devotion to his business; and the attainment of a million dollars may seem to him an attainment glorious beyond all other attainments. It is not difficult to see that such a man would go ahead with the struggle for this object. But the second man, equally farsighted, may be by nature more indolent, or, though possessed of equal energy, he may have a wider range of interests; he may like pictures, music, literature, philosophy, travel or women; the ambition for a million dollars may seem to him a ridiculous and childish ambition; he may feel that an income of $7,500 a year suffices for all his needs. It is not difficult to see that for him the price attached to amassing a million dollars would seem prohibitive, and the end not worth the gaining.

But we must pass from this consideration of what men do and do not want, to the question of what they ought or ought not to want. Of two men, that man who has the more ambition, who is prepared to make the greater sacrifices, must be admitted to have the more will-power; but he is not necessarily the more admirable character. I am all for ambition and success, but what I remonstrate against is the particular kind of ambition and success which is usually held up to the young man of today to emulate. It is usually narrow and material, and nearly always selfish. A man ought to set himself a high goal and he ought to attach a high value to that goal. Further, he ought not to attach too much importance to obstacles and sacrifices; he should welcome these as challenges to test his mettle. But the goal must be great enough to make the obstacles and sacrifices worth while; and it may be questioned whether a purely material and selfish goal does that.

What ought a man's goal to be? Stated in the most abstract terms, it ought to be (beyond the mere duty of making himself happy) to increase social well-being to confer the greatest benefits he can upon humanity. But instead of this, what do nine-tenths of the Success writers exhort us to do? They point to the great material successes, the men who have gathered in more engraved paper than other men, the men who have attained fame; and they tell us to ape such as these. It is true that a very large number of Successful Men, in the process of attaining money and fame, have incidentally conferred benefits upon mankind. That is one of the ways of acquiring money and fame. In order to "get ahead," you may work harder than the man at the desk beside you; you may study at home, you may be more efficient, you may devise plans for saving the firm money; you may patent an invention. And by these methods, adopted primarily that you yourself may get ahead, you are adding to your productivity; you are increasing the world's supply of goods and services; you are conferring benefits upon mankind. Though your end is selfish, you are compelled to help others in order to attain it. In order to persuade people to give you a lot of money, you are obliged to confer equivalent benefits upon them.

"But if the pursuit of what you call material and narrow and selfish ends leads to all these beneficial results," some one may ask, "what objections can you possibly have to them?" My objections, my dear sir, is simply this. So long as fame and money are the ends sought, the benefits conferred upon humanity are mere by-products; whereas, in any civilization worthy of the name, the ends sought by individuals ought to be social well-being, and fame and money the by-products. When money is the end sought, and social well-being merely the bi-product, we produce more money than we need and not enough well-being. We over-eat and over-dress and turn out mountains of silly luxuries; we seek to outdo our neighbors in material display; while the enrichment of the mind and the elevation of the soul are ignored, or occupy us only in moments when we have nothing else to do.

Material wealth is all very well in its way; a certain amount of it is an indispensable preliminary to any culture of the spirit whatever; unless a man has enough to eat, his brain will not for very long be able to function. But after we have acquired enough wealth to live in comfort (which does not include silly competitive display), we ought to turn to higher and better things. I feel like shouting; For God's sake, man, can't you see that the acquisition of wealth is a means and not an end?

It is further and finally to be said that the man whose sole ambition is to accumulate wealth (and even to do so honestly), must give people what they want and not necessarily what is good for them. A theatrical manager can gather a fortune by staging salacious plays. There is a moving picture actor with an irresistibly funny way of wiggling his feet. He acquires hundreds of thousands of dollars a year for making people laugh; while college professors starve for trying to make people think.

Yet after all this, there is something to be said for the ordinary selfish ambition. It is vastly better than no ambition at all. Though the benefits it confers on others may be incidental, it does confer them; and those benefits; even if they are usually material, are often vast. The world would be a very meager place if we lost our selfish ambitions without acquiring altruistic ambitions in their stead. And from the standpoint of will-power, which is, after all, our present subject, there is a very great deal to be said for selfish ambitions. Huxley, in his lecture on Scientific Education, happens to have said this so well that I cannot do better than quote his words:

> I do not wish it to be supposed that, because I happen to be devoted to more or less abstract and "unpractical" pursuits, I am insensible to the weight which ought to be attached to that which has been said to be the English conception of Paradise; namely, "getting on." I look upon it that "getting on" is a very important matter indeed. I do not mean merely for the sake of the coarse and tangible results of success, but because humanity is so constituted that a vast number of us would never be impelled to those stretches of exertion which make us wiser and more capable men, if it were not for the absolute necessity of putting on our faculties all the strain they will bear, for the purpose of "getting on" in the most practical sense.

VIII
CONTROLLING ONE'S THOUGHTS

AFTER this ethical interlude on life's ideals, perhaps we had better take our bearing again. We have seen that whatever our ideals, whatever our resolutions, we should, before adopting those resolutions, calmly and coldly count the price of carrying them out. That was our first rule of will-power.

Now the second rule follows naturally from the first. Once you have made your decision, having coldly decided that that is what you want and that you are willing to pay the price, your decision is forever beyond dispute. You should never ask yourself again whether the other course is possible; whether it is really worth while staying home to study for a specified number of evenings each week; whether a man who has resolved to stop drinking can really do so suddenly without blowing to pieces; whether smoking is really as harmful as you had thought it was; whether a man in a moderate position, without so many responsibilities and burdens on his shoulders, doesn't really get just as much enjoyment out of life as the Success. Those questions are forever closed; you have asked them before and have decided them. You will know that thoughts determine action, and to control your actions you will begin by controlling your thought. You will vivify all the advantages that will come from carrying out your resolution. You will paint them in glowing colors. You will dwell on them constantly. The disadvantages you will ignore. They are disadvantages only to fools; a wise man does not think them so.

Here I need to give a warning. Concentrate on the positive side; avoid the negative. That is, dwell on the benefits of carrying your resolve out, not on the evils of failing. If you would fight a craving for morphine, do not let your imagination revel in the picture of the ashen-faced, palsied, loathsome and pitiable creature you would be as a morphine fiend. Picture the upstanding, energetic, healthy-complexioned, respect-compelling man you are going to be if you refuse it.

A morbid, terrible picture is a mind-filling picture; it exerts a strange fascination. If a thought once sufficiently fills the mind, be it ever so terrible, unreasonable or self-destructive, it will be acted upon. I need merely cite the familiar experience of dizziness when looking over a precipice or a high building, or even a low building if there be no rail around. The height from sea-level has nothing to do with it; and the height of the potential fall is less important than the actual danger of falling. You grow dizzy because you think of what would happen to you if you lost your balance and fell, or even if you were to throw yourself off. The higher the roof or precipice the more fascinating does this idea become; hence the greater the dizziness. It is the very terror of the thought, the reality of the fear that you are going to act upon it, that makes you dizzy. If you could get completely rid of the idea, you would completely lose the dizziness. I knew a man living in Buffalo who did not dare to visit Niagara Falls, lest he should throw himself into the magnificent rapids just above them. There are doubtless many like him.

Fill the mind with the positive idea of your resolve, and you will carry it out.

Some readers will have recognized an affinity between this rule and the doctrine known as "suggestion." Little is yet known of suggestion, but enough is known for scientific men to become assured that it is no more superstition; practicing physicians recognize its great value. One writer, T. Sharper Knowlson, convinced of the theory, has made some pointed remarks on the subject:

> We have not to aim at a strong will, and wait until it "comes." Act as if it had already come. . . . The man who feels he cannot pass a public house without an irresistible temptation to enter and drink to excess, must tell himself he *can*, and proceed to walk past the place of temptation.

He suggests a method for combating insomnia. One should say to oneself, "I sleep, I sleep," repeating these words until a state of drowsiness is induced. "It is wrong to say, "I shall sleep,' because that implies desire, and hence a possibility of non-fulfillment. Suggestion works by affirmation, not by promise."

My next piece of advice is this: Never defy temptation—evade it.

You may look upon this advice as inconsistent with the above quotation. You may dismiss it as unworthy. I maintain that it is prudent. For urging it I have the strongest psychologic grounds.

In one of his studies in pessimism, Schopenhauer makes a remark to the effect that man has thousands of desires, and as at any moment not more than a few of them are fulfilled, man's existence must necessarily always be miserable. Schopenhauer could only arrive at a conclusion so opposed to common sense because his psychology was defective. Desires are not ever-present. Desires are like thoughts—they *are* thoughts—that come and go. They are aroused by association and suggestion, and less apt to appear when there is no association or suggestion to call them up.

I walk along the street. I am, so far as I am consciously aware, content; which is the same thing as being so. But I pass a fruit-stand; I espy some delicious peaches, and there is immediately aroused the desire for peaches. The absence of the fruit then produces in me a maw, which must be filled. When I watch an exhibition tennis match, my desire to become a marvelous player is intense. When I go to a skating rink, I attach great value to the personal achievement of expert skating. When I read a book on the history of metaphysics, I desire to become a great philosopher. When I listen to speeches in the midst of a presidential campaign, I fancy that the one thing worthwhile is to become an eminent statesman. Between campaigns, this ambition falls into the background. If I have not been skating for a long time, my desire for preeminence in it fades.

The moral of all this, on its positive side, is to cultivate most your desires for the activities which will best forward your final purposes—those purposes which you have calmly, deliberately and fully reasoned out. On the negative side, the moral is to avoid all associations, suggestions, lines of thought, which arouse desires that interfere with your final purposes, that is to say, desires that you have resolved against.

The drunkard often has little difficulty in keeping straight until he sees liquor; even then he is better able to resist than after he has scented or tasted liquor. If you have resolved forever to cease drinking, do not, to show the strength of your determination, as people do in motion picture dramas, put the red glass to your lips and then set it down. Putting the glass to your lips is liable to be your undoing. Do not raise the glass. DO not order the drink. Do not enter the saloon. If the saloon is directly in line on your way home, and habit has dictated your entrance, walk a block out of the way if necessary.

Mr. Knowlson says that you should tell yourself you can walk past, and then do it. That is all very well for the later stages, but I fancy you will find that suggestion and self-faith have their greatest value when not over strained. You cannot lift a 500-pound weight at arm's length by telling yourself you can. But by gradual exercises, adding a little bit each week, a man may develop a physique which may enable him to accomplish marvels he never dreamed of before. **And the will is just like that. It must be developed slowly.**

This is not my discovery. Bacon discovered it some three centuries ago, and though his language is somewhat antiquated, his wisdom is as wise today as on the day it was written:

> He that seeketh victory over his nature, let him not set himself too great nor too small tasks; for the first will make him dejected by often failings, and the second will make him a small proceeder, though by often prevailings. And, as the first, let him practice with helps, as swimmers do with bladders, or rushes; but after a time let him practice with disadvantages as dancers do with thick shoes; for it breeds great perfection if the practice be harder than the use.

Therefore it is better to walk around the block a while, if you must, before going past. Then you may have faith; and your faith will be strengthened by the modest record of avoidance behind you.

This alcoholic illustration, as I have indicated before, may be legally obsolete; but it is sufficient to indicate to a reader fertile in ideas the application of the principle to any other instance.

IX
THE OMNIPRESENCE OF HABIT

THUS far I have spoken as if desires (and fears and aversions) were the sole determinants of action. We come now to something quite as important, if, indeed, it is not more important than these. While it is often determined by them, it sometimes determines them, and it often guides action with no relation to desires whatever. From the title of this chapter, the astute reader will have already surmised what I am talking about.

We may best approach the phenomenon of habit by going outside of the individual and his brain. Habit applies to the inanimate no less than to the animate world. Fold a napkin in a particular way and it is more easy to fold that way the next time. The creases in a sheet of wrapping paper become indelible. An automobile engine runs more smoothly after it has been "worked in," and the friction edges word down. The very clothes on your back form habits; they fit you better after you have worn them for some time than when they are new; they drape more snugly to the form. The notorious difference in comfort between old and new shoes is possible because the old shoes have been worked into certain feet-conforming habits. A path across a field, be it ever so winding, becomes beaten more and more, becomes more distinct and unalterable. That is because it becomes more and more the path of least resistance. And the tendency of all bodies and forces, animate and inanimate, to follow the path of least resistance, is the secret of the formation of habit.

You assert that the field path is formed by human beings, creatures of habit, the beaten path and of ruts. I answer by the illustration of a river bed, which the water follows, though the bed twist and turn and wind. Originally it was formed by sheer accident, as the water, beginning as a spring on a hill or mountain top, bubbled up, made its way around this rock and over that, split here, joined there, washing away the gravel as it went, digging its bed deeper and deeper, more firm and more unchangeable, till at last it flowed in a full, deep, untroubled current. You have doubtless seen the bed of a spring or brook dried up at certain seasons of the year. The definition of a brook is a body of water; yet you know, though there is no water here, that this is indeed the brook, for this is the path the water will take when it flows again. The dried-up brook-bed represents what a habit is like in the brain when you are not acting upon it.

A more familiar comparison to those who live in the world created by man and not by nature is the groove in a phonograph record—silent in itself, but always ready to produce a tune, and always the same tune, when it is put on; that is to say, when the circumstances call if forth.

The omnipresence of habit is almost terrifying when one reflects upon it. From the minute a man shuts off his alarm clock on one morning, till the minute he shuts it off on the next morning, it controls him. It dictates and makes possible nine-tenths of his actions. And nine-tenths of the habits of most men are formed unconsciously. It is astounding that men should so leave this thing to chance, when it determines the very texture of their lives; yet the fact must be recorded.

A man gets up at eight because it is his habit to get up at eight, though he has set his alarm and his intentions to arise at half-past seven. If it is his habit in a vacant way to contemplate getting up for fifteen minutes before he actually does get up, that he will do every morning. When he actually gets up, habit dictates which sock shall go on first, whether shirt or trousers shall go on first, whether collar or shoes shall take precedence, which shoe shall be put on before the other, whether he begins buttoning his vest from the bottom or from the top.

At this very private stage of his toilet we shall leave him a moment for a digression. This digression is needed to point out that habit is not always evil. The same confusion of thought exists in regard to habit, and about being a "slave to habit," that clusters around the word "Desire." Most of the average man's habits are not only good but indispensable. Habit may be formally defined as an aptitude or inclination for some action, acquired by frequent repetition, and showing itself in increased facility of performance or in decreased power of resistance. Less correctly but more practically, I should define habit as the doing of a thing without conscious attention and often without thought of the purpose of doing it. Most men cannot tell you how they dress, which shoe they put on first, or whether they button their vests from the top or bottom, until they first mentally rehearse the action or even until they actually do it.

As to the great blessings of habit, Dr. Maudsley says:

> If an act became no easier after being done several times, if the careful direction of consciousness were necessary to its accomplishment on each occasion, it is evident that the whole activity of a lifetime might be confined to one or two deeds—that no progress could take place in development. A man might be occupied all day in dressing and undressing himself; the attitude of his body would absorb all his attention and energy; the washing of his hands or the fastening of a button would be as difficult to him on each occasion as to the child on its first trial; and

he would, further more, be completely exhausted by his exertions. Think of the pains necessary to teach a child to stand of the many efforts which it must make, and of the ease with which it at last stands, unconscious of any effort.

Returning now to our typical man and his morning toilet, we follow him downstairs to his breakfast. Habit dictates what he eats, whether his breakfast is light or heavy, whether he takes a cereal or not, whether his fried eggs are turned or not. Habit has already dictated what time he usually arrives at breakfast; it must, therefore, inevitably dictate whether he shall bolt his breakfast or take it leisurely. Habit dictates whether he props his paper in front of him at breakfast or whether he waits until he boards his train. Habit dictates his table manners. Habit dictates his tone of voice to his wife. If he boards a train, habit dictates whether he shall get on the rear car or the second car from the front. Arrived at his office, habit dictates the manner in which he approaches his work, the way he handles interviews, his professional mannerisms, his tricks of gesture, his choice of words, his very manner of thinking and way of looking at things. Habit dictates the time he goes out to lunch, and the place to which he goes. Many a man with a special luncheon engagement at an inhabitable place has suddenly checked himself to remember it, after finding that his feet had mysteriously carried him right up to the very door of his customary restaurant!

Finally, when he has returned home and taken his dinner, habit dictates how he shall spend the evening. If he is in the habit of going out every night, he will feel restless and uncomfortable staying in. He will go out not for enjoyment, but because he knows not what else to do. He knows merely that the thought of staying home is intolerable. His so-called pleasures, far from spontaneous, fall into certain conventionalized and accepted activities, which may be called social habits, habits possessed by the community at large. They will differ between one country and another, between one town in the same country and another. Our man will find himself for a period going frequently out to play poker; then for another period he will find his most frequent diversion will be going to dances; for a while it will be going to the theatre or the "movies"; for another period it may be bowling; then it will be staying at home to read. Such habits change with seasons, by sheer accident, and in different periods of life. The evenings of some men are as much a burden to them as their business day. Their evening's outing is as much a duty as earning their bread and cheese. As they dress to go out, they sigh. They are about to embark on one of the accredited methods of "having a good time"; it often does not occur to them to ask whether they are actually having it. They vaguely regard going out as a sort of necessity, like Fate. They are indeed slaves of habit.

But our man's day is not ended. He returns home. Habit dictates the hour at which he retires, even though he has made a thousand resolutions, night after night, that he shall hereafter retire an hour earlier. In fact, the nightly resolution itself may be a habit. The resolution is usually made in the morning; for an outside influence (his employer or the relentless call of business) has pretty definitely fixed the hour at which he must arise. His manner of undressing is as definitely fixed as his manner of dressing. He puts out the light, opens the window and goes to bed. Habit dictates the position he assumes in bed, and perhaps how deeply he sleeps or fails to sleep...

We have pursued our typical man enough, and we leave him. There are worse than he. Absentminded persons, not accustomed to changing their dress to go out of an evening, and intending only to take off a few articles, have found themselves getting completely undressed, and proceeding to go to bed.

You who laugh irreverently at this, who boast that you are free from unthinking habit, and that you act only with thought, kindly make this experiment. Perhaps you carry your watch in your lower right-hand vest pocket, the chain across your vest, your keys or knife or ornament in the other pocket on the end of the chain. Reverse it; put your watch in your lower left-hand pocket. Now, without making any special effort either to forget or to remember that you have shifted your watch, wait until an unplanned occasion to use it arises, and see how many times you reach in your right-hand pocket for it and pull out the other end of the chain before finally a new habit is formed. Or put your watch in your upper pocket, and see how many times you reach for your lower pocket and think frantically for a moment that your watch is gone. Or shift your silver change from your trousers to your coat pocket, or from your right to your left, and see how many times the wrong hand dives into the wrong place!

Habit makes possible the acquisition of all skilled movement. The practice that makes perfect, the practice at swimming, tennis, skating, dancing, bowling, juggling, automobile driving and stunting with an airplane, is nothing more and nothing less than the formation of habit. I have learned to operate a typewriter by touch. As I write these words, I do not have to pick out the letters on the keyboard. I do not look at the keyboard. I do not even think of the letters. I think only of what I am going to say; I watch the words on the paper as they marvelously form; and my fingers, without attention from me, are mysteriously finding their way with lightning rapidity to the proper keys. Habit! And if I should start to think consciously of my fingers or the keys, I should begin to make mistakes and my speed would slow up.

If you are still not sufficiently impressed with the importance of habit, let me quote to you the words, not of a moralist given to sermonizing, but the dry scientific statement of fact by a psychologist, W.B. Pillsbury:

> The useful man is for the greater part marked off from the useless and the vicious by the nature of his habits. Industry or indolence, good temper or bad temper, even virtue or vice, are in the last analysis largely matters of habit. One forms the habit of working at certain times of the day, and soon if one is not busy at that time one experiences a lively sense of discomfort. Or, on the contrary, one forms the habit of loafing all day. Work then becomes distasteful and indolent irresponsibility is established. Losing one's temper is largely a habit, as is self control. Each time one is provoked by a trifle, it becomes the more difficult to look calmly at an unpleasant episode; while each time one remains calm under difficult circumstances, strength is gained for later difficulties. Similarly, whenever temptation is resisted, virtue gains a victory; when temptation is yielded to, new weaknesses develop. Frequent yielding makes resistance practically impossible. A bank president of established morals could no more step out and pick a pocket that was temptingly unprotected than he could fly. The habitual drunkard can no more resist the invitation to have a glass than he can resist the action of gravitation while falling freely through space. Frequent giving in has entirely destroyed his original freedom of choice.

X
THE ALTERATION OF HABIT

HABIT being of such enormous importance, it is our urgent duty to seek the means of forming good habits and of breaking bad ones.

How does habit become possible? For the answer to that, one must turn to the strange and awe-compelling mass of gray and white matter boxed within the bones of the skull. The brain is composed of an immense number of separate and minute cells, called "neurons." Each is connected potentially with a number of other neurons. The points of connection are called "synapses." We may visualize the brain as a network of delicate piping or exquisitely slender tubes, each tube containing a number of valves leading to other tubes. The tubes are the neurons; the valves the synapses. When a stimulus comes from the outside world, it sends a mysterious current, which we may envisage as the current of some fluid, like water, through one of the tubes; this forces itself out of one of the valves into the particular tube leading from that valve; this tube in turn has a number of valves, and the current forces its way out of the one most easily opened, and so on, until the current emerges finally in the form of an action. In this picture I have represented as tubes nerves as well as neurons. The tubes which send incoming messages to the brain are called "sensory" nerves; those which carry out the orders of the brain are called "motor" nerves.

If the outward stimulus is an itch, the message is carried by an adjacent sensory nerve to the brain, passes through the tubes and vale, the neurons and synapses, and emerges through a motor nerve in the form of the action of scratching. Or, the itch is discovered by some nerve in the eye to be due to a scab, which it would be harmful to scratch. This nerve sets up a counter current; other valves are opened, and others kept closed, and the action of scratching does not follow. Certain valves, or synapses, are from birth predisposed to open with particular ease. The special paths which these make possible are called instincts. The infant feeds on its mother's breast at birth. It has had no experience, no knowledge; it may not be able to see. Yet a particular sensation awakens a particular response. The instincts we have in common. In addition to these inherited paths which all have, there are paths open in the brain at birth which vary in different individuals. These we call innate characteristics.

Now while these paths of instinct and innate characteristics are often highly useful, they are sometimes exceedingly dangerous. They need to be supplemented by experience and knowledge, which dictate the opening of new or altered paths. When a path is once taken, it wears down the valves, the synapses, through which it passes. Those valves open so much the easier thereafter, and the taking of that path becomes so much easier the next time. On the next passage of the current those particular synapses open more easily still, until the time may come when they will form the only possible path, when it will be impossible for the well-worn valve to offer more resistance to the on-rushing current than the valve seldom or never opened.

Such is the physiologist's explanation of habit, and it is at once a despair and a glorious promise. Forming a new habit is like forging for yourself a new path in the woods, through stubborn underbrush and prickly thorns, while all the while it is possible for you to take the well-worn, hard-trodden, pleasant path that already exists. But you can reflect that every time you travel through the new path you are going to tramp down more shrubbery and clear more entanglements from the way. Every time you take the path it is going to become easier.

And that is the cheerful side. When you first set about to abolish a bad habit and establish a good one, it is going to take all the effort, all the "will-power," at your command. But habit begins soon to take the place of will-power; it will require less and less effort, less and less will-power, each time; the strain diminishes, until in time it disappears. For the practice of that particular virtue, will-power has become almost useless. Will-power is not needed all the time. It is called for only at the period of change.

But the period of change is all-important. It is better not to be too ambitious, and not to try to change too many habits at once. Yet as soon as you find one new method of response becoming automatic, you may turn to another. You will always find another. No matter how long you live nor how diligent you are, you will never exhaust the supply of new good habits that it is possible to form, nor the supply of old bad habits it is possible to break. And all the time you will be keeping alive the faculty of effort within you. Putting forth moral effort, or failing to is itself a habit.

All this comes under the head of what William James would call *making our nervous system our ally instead of our enemy*, which consists in making automatic and habitual, as early as possible, as many useful actions as we can. James, building on the suggestions of Bain, has laid down several maxims of habit which it would be difficult to improve upon:

> The first is that in the acquisition of a new habit, or the leaving off of an old one, we must take care to *launch ourselves with as strong and decided an initiative as*

possible. Accumulate all the possible circumstances which shall re-enforce the right motives; put yourself assiduously in conditions that encourage the new way; make engagements incompatible with the old; take a public pledge; if the case allows; in short, envelop your resolution with every aid you know. This will give your new beginning such a momentum that the temptation to break down will not occur as it otherwise might; and every day during which a breakdown is postponed adds to the chances of its not occurring at all.

In this connection let me say a word about the effect of a change of environment upon a change of habit. In our ordinary life a certain routine is laid down for us from without, and this largely controls the routine developed from within. Our hours of business and the hours at which we take our meals, the time it takes to get from the office to the home and the method that must be taken, the very arrangement of furniture in our room, all help to engender and develop and petrify certain habits. But if a break should occur in this routine, if the hours or the nature of our business should be changed, if we should move from the city to the country, a vast number of our habits would be changed perforce. Such changes in environment should be welcomed when they occur; they should be recognized and seized upon as rare opportunities for the conscious formation of new useful habits and the breaking of old bad ones. The old habits were made possible because they were unconsciously suggested by associations in the old environment. But when we change, we can no longer do some of the old things absent-mindedly, because the old responses are not suggested, and often they do not fit. Reform in our habits of rising and retiring, in the hasty or leisurely eating of our meals, and many other daily custom that determines our life happiness, thus becomes more possible. But the trouble is that most of us, when such opportunities come, fail to appreciate them, and fall again unconsciously, without deliberate choice, into habits as bad as the habits we left.

Returning to the James-Bain maxims, the second is:

> *Never suffer an exception to occur till the new habit is securely rooted in your life.* Each lapse is like the letting fall of a ball of string which one is carefully winding up; a single slip undoes more than a great many turns will wind again. *Continuity* of training is the great means of making the nervous system act infallibly right.

A German writer has remarked: "He who every day makes a fresh resolve is like one who, arriving at the edge of the ditch he is to leap, forever stops and returns for a fresh run."

This leads to James's third maxim, which is:

> *Seize the very first possible opportunity to act on every resolution you make, and on every emotional prompting you may experience in the direction of the habits you aspire to gain.* It is not in the moment of their forming, but in the moment of their producing motor effects, that resolves and aspirations communicate the new "set" to the brain. No matter how full a reservoir of maxims one may posses, and no matter how good one's sentiments may be, if one has not taken advantage of every concrete opportunity to act, one's character may remain entirely unaffected for the better.

And to impress his remarks, James gives a final example:

> The drunken Rip Van Winkle, in Jefferson's play, excuses himself for every fresh dereliction by saying, "I won't count this time!" Well he may not count it, and a kind Heaven may not count it; but it is being counted none the less. Down among his nerve-cells and fibers the molecules are counting it, registering and storing it up to be used against him when the next temptation comes. Nothing we ever do is, in strict scientific literalness wiped out.

Oh, the pathos of telling yourself, when each new temptation arises: "I will begin to reform the *next* time. I will yield this time, and this will be the last." Oh, the tragedy of that excuse! Self-deception could not possibly be more complete. If you can only tell yourself, when temptations arises, not that *this* time will be the last, but that the *last* time was the last! If you can only repeat that to yourself, if you can force your attention to rivet on that fact, if you can only realize that the whole force of your will and moral effort must be summoned *now* and not at some vague time in the future, if you can burn into your mind that *this* battle, *this* inward struggle against temptation, is the only real and crucial one, if you can forget about the moral struggles won or lost in the past or that you expect to win in the future, and concentrate only upon the *present* battle, then truly you will be on the way to will-power. And it is the only way. Moral sentiments, fine ideals, excellent mottoes, splendid resolutions, are all mere preparation for the struggle. They are all very well in their place, but if they do not express themselves in *action*, and express themselves at the moment when temptation has come, they are worse than useless.

There was once a man whose wife, for curious reasons, was beaten by another man. This beating occurred regularly. The other man would break into the house, flog the wife unmercifully in front of the husband until she fell unconscious, and then leave. The other man was bigger than the husband, so the husband could not fight back. But the husband bought himself a revolver. It was a beautiful revolver, with an exquisite pearl handle, and its nickel finish glistened in the sun. The husband loaded it. The other man came again, beat the man's wife until she screamed for mercy, and left her prostrate. "But where was the husband?" you ask. He was right on the scene. "Didn't he use his revolver?" you persist. Well, the fact must be admitted that a very strange thing happened. When the other man came, the husband was so frightened that he dropped his revolver and ran. This happened again and again. It may be said to the husband's credit, however, that every time the beating was over, and the other man had left, the husband always came back; picked up his revolver, petted it lovingly, polished it again, pointed it with magnificent determination at an imaginary object, and said, "Ah, wait till he comes *next* time."

This is a parable. It is hardly necessary to point out that the other man symbolizes the man's temptations and cravings and baser instincts, that the wife symbolizes his better self, that the revolver symbolizes his ideals, and the cartridges his sentiments and mottoes and resolutions. In the moment when they were needed, these cartridges did not "go off," they did not explode, they were not effective, and the simple reason was that the man did not summon the effort to pull the trigger. You need ask yourself only one question about this parable, but your answer must be honest: "Does the husband symbolize Me?"

XI
WILL AND THE PSYCHOANALYSTS

PRACTICALLY within the last few years there has grown up a body of doctrine, gradually becoming surrounded with a formidable literature, which its proponents call a "science"; and I shall not start an argument at the very beginning by denying its title to that word. This body of doctrine is called "psychoanalysis." It is not quite clear whether its adherents consider it a branch of psychology or a competitor. But at all events, it has just now become ubiquitous. It is in the air. It is the fad. It has come out of the laboratories into the drawing rooms, out of the consulting rooms into the newspapers. It is discussed by doctors and book-reviewers and spinsters and school girls. It deals with human action, with the mind, the will, the desires, it lays down recommendations; and any modern book upon the will, though it may embrace or damn psychoanalysis, cannot afford to ignore it.

Now it is very difficult to pass fair judgment upon this body of doctrine. It is so young. It has already, to my mind, made not unimportant steps in the treatment and cure of insanity and nervous diseases, and bids fair to make greater. Its theories of multiple personalities and the meaning of dreams seem to me fruitful working hypotheses, determined to add to the achievements of psychiatry. Its explanations of Puritanism and of certain phases of war psychology, utterly apart from the question of whether or not they have scientific value, are delicious and effective bits of satire; and, as with Thorstein Veblen's work in economics, the satire is heightened, not diminished, by the dry, scientific vocabulary in which it is wrapped and the impartial scientific attitude which it affects.

Psychoanalysis, doubtless, is proceeding on many wrong theories, and as time goes on the bad will cast upon the scrap-heap and new and better theories substituted. It is tapping and specializing upon a vein which the academic psychology had neglected. It has attracted wide popular interest. It has brought controversy into psychology; and controversy, with experiments to prove or disprove, always means life and growth and progress, and is the enemy of stagnation. It is true that the literature of psychoanalysis is morbid, gruesome, depressing; filled with sexual perversions, with incest, sadism, masochism, onanism, sodomy; but what would you? Medical books on physical diseases are also horrible—but necessary. Spiritual scabs and ravages and pus are more revolting than physical—but like the physical, if we are to combat them, we must study them with the cold detached impartiality of the physician. We must for the moment put aside our moral platitudes and denunciations and contempt and study the disease and its cure. The physician does not denounce his patient for becoming ill, though the patient may well deserve it. He seeks first to restore health. Admonition can only follow.

But when I have said all this in favor of psychoanalysis, I have said almost as much as I conscientiously can. Few of its practitioners are well-grounded in psychology, and fewer in biology and medicine. It utilizes orthodox medicine, biology, psychology, anatomy and physiology when they can be used to prove a special point, and rejects them when they can not. There is hardly a single analyst who could be called a cautious thinker. Most of them do not appear to know the difference between a substantiated theory and a guess. Presumptive evidence is set down as if it were conclusive evidence. Some of their deductions are highly fanciful. They would be extremely difficult to verify, and there is usually no attempt at verification. Whenever human nature is praised, proof is required, but apparently whenever it is satirized or insulted, proof is deemed superfluous. The most dubious conjecture, based on the frailest kind of evidence, is set down with the positive air of a fact. Explanations for which the best that can be said is that they are possible or plausible are treated as if they were the final and only ones; though alternative explanations, at least equally and possibly more plausible, and certainly nowhere near as far-fetched, may occur to a person not altogether hypnotized by the Freudian interpretation.

It is one of the foremost Freudian theories—if indeed, it is not the foremost—that every dream (not *some* dreams, mind you, but every one!) represents the gratification of some desire suppressed or repressed during the waking state. This desire, according to Freud, is practically always a sexual one; at least the predominance of the sexual element appears to be overwhelming.

Now such a theory in its bald state would not impose upon a half-witted person. So the psychoanalysts go on to show that most of our dreams are "symbolic." And what ingenious symbolism! The unconscious mind asleep seems to me infinitely more clever than the couscous mind awake! It is also a theory of Freud's that every act, every slip of the tongue, every bit of absent-mindedness or forgetfulness, means something. Forgetting a name, an event or a figure, is not merely failure to remember; it is a positive act. We forget because we have an unconscious desire to forget; the fact or name is associated with something unpleasant and the mind tends to eject it or the unconscious to suppress it. I wish I had time, for your edification, to quote a few typical examples of the "interpretations" which the psychoanalysts give of different dreams and trivial acts in the light of these theories.

Their capacity for reading anything they choose into anything they want is utterly enormous. You would sometimes think from a few of these "interpretations" that the psychoanalysts were satirizing or burlesquing themselves. Really it is not so. But the reader who has sufficient psychologic curiosity to be interested in seeing how a theory can be ridden to death and then pulled to its feet and ridden again would find unsurpassed material by delving a little into psychoanalytic literature.

A large part of the interest in psychoanalysis is almost wholly prurient. It is to the fact that it deals so largely with "sex" I verily believe, that it owes the largely part of its popular vogues. It seems, too, to have a certain tendency to wallow in it and find a morbid fascination in it. Examples of sexual abnormalities are piled up with a relish not unlike that which gossiping people have in retailing scandal, and often apparently with the same object—to tell the tale for the sake of the tale. The examples are usually more than are needed to enforce a given conclusion, though the exact bearing of each upon the conclusion is not always indicated.

There can be little doubt that the reading of psychoanalytic literature tends to suggest and arouse sexual trains of thought in the minds of many readers, and I am here speaking of "normal" readers, and not of what the psychoanalysts would call a "sexually hypersensitive" or "hyperaesthetic" reader. The same, of course, may be true of a medical book. I am not condemning. I am merely stating a fact.

This statement has been made before, and one psychoanalyst has attempted to answer it in this wise: "The sexual material is present in every subject, normal or abnormal, and comes to the surface very easily. No suggestion is necessary to bring it forth."

That is emphatically not an answer. We have seen before, in our inquiry into the nature of desire, that desires are not ever-present, but become active only when some train of though or some external observation or stimulus has aroused them; and we illustrated by a phonograph record, which, while it preserves a tune, is silent when it isn't being played. The example of passing the fruit-stand was given as a case in point. The like is true of sexual desires. Whether a desire "comes to the surface" or stays below is a point of very great importance.

The psychoanalytic method is incomplete, insufficiently checked up by other methods, and rests upon some dubious assumptions. It seeks to interpret the normal mind through a study of the abnormal mind. This is a perfectly valid and useful method within proper limits, but it can be overdone and rashly handled. "The neurotic," says one psychoanalyst, "only accentuates certain general human traits and tendencies and he makes them, thereby, easier to observe." Such a statement needs qualification. Instead of "accentuating" a trait of a normal man, the neurotic may be a neurotic because he so greatly distorts it. Disease symptoms do not "accentuate" health symptoms.

Finally, to all these sins, psychoanalysis adds the unforgivable crime of pedantry. I do not know of a science that habitually wraps its thoughts in such awesome and jawcracking phraseology, with such a maze of newly coined words, above all, habitually tacking on the magic word "complex" after describing any train whatever in order to make it sound as if something very profound had been pointed out. When most of these psychoanalytic thoughts are disentangled from the verbiage in which they are snarled and concealed, and lie before you in all their nakedness, they are seen to be either very commonplace and obvious, or very absurd. Such a discovery might be suspected in advance, for poverty of thought habitually tries to conceal itself beneath a deluge of diction. This may be a case of the "unconscious" or the "inferiority complex," forming a "self-protective neurosis!"

But this is digressing. My purpose is not to criticize psychoanalysis as a whole, but to examine one of its cardinal doctrines which seems to me to bear directly on the subject of will-power. But first I shall have to explain what that doctrine is.

The psychoanalysts lay a good deal of stress upon what is commonly called the subconscious, and what they call the unconscious. Their conception of the unconscious is vividly described by Mr. André Tridon, in a book on *Psychoanalysis and Behavior*, from which I shall take the liberty of quoting:

> Our unconscious "contains" two sorts of "thoughts"; those which rise easily to the surface of our consciousness and those which remain at the bottom and can only be made to rise with more or less difficulty.
>
> Our unconscious mind is like a pool into which dead leaves, dust, rain drops and a thousand other things are falling day after day, some of them floating on the surface for a while, some sinking to the bottom and, all of them, after a while, merging themselves with the water or the ooze. Let us suppose that two dead dogs, one of them weighted down with a stone, have been thrown into that pool. They will poison the water, and people wishing to use those waters will have to rake the ooze and remove the rotting carrion. The dog whose body was not fastened to any heavy object will easily be brought to the surface and removed. The other will be more difficult to recover, and if the stone is very heavy, may remain in the pool until ways and means are devised to dismember him or to cut the rope holding him down.

Now these two dogs may be made to represent two sorts of desires or cravings. The first of these are cravings of which we are aware, but which, because they are "immoral" or socially detrimental, or difficult or impossible to gratify for some other reason, remain unacted upon. These are called "suppressed" desires. The second are cravings which we not only fail to gratify, but of whose very existence we are unaware. If someone were to suggest that we had such cravings we might even vehemently, and perhaps honestly, deny it. These are called "repressed" desires.

Now, say the psychoanalysts, though we cannot suppress or repress our cravings, we cannot annihilate them. To use one of their similes: "Whether we remain in ignorance of the fact that a boiler is full of steam or simply disregard that fact, the steam is there, seeking an outlet and likely to create an abnormal one, unless a normal outlet is provided."

What will this "abnormal outlet" be? According to the psychoanalysts, it may take several forms. "Between the compelling instinct and the opposing force of sexual denial," for instance, "the way is prepared for some disturbance which does not solve the conflict but seeks to escape it by changing the libidinous cravings into symptoms of disease." In other words, the suppression or repression of sexual cravings, they assert, will lead to anxiety dreams, nightmares, nervous disorders, intolerance, hallucinations, dual and multiple personalities, insanity, or burst out in abnormal sexual perversions of a revolting sort. They bring forth examples of perversions in great men. They point with a finger of warning at the ascetics and holy men and women who were fighting the flesh, and contend that these exchanged normal reality for hallucinations, and normal desires for perverse desires.

And what cure do they suggest? Here I must be cautious, and warn the reader that the psychoanalysts do not altogether agree upon this matter among themselves. I will try, however, as best I may, to do justice to the bulk of their opinion.

They believe, first, that we should be made conscious of our repressed cravings. To make the subject conscious of these, they interpret his acts, study his dreams, unravel the symbolism, and gradually inform the patient what his repressed cravings are. This is cutting the rope that holds the dead dog down. The first job is to bring him to the surface.

Critics have feared that causing these unconscious cravings to rise to consciousness may cause them to overpower the patient's ethical strivings. The belief has also been expressed that this method may suggest a craving or put into the mind of the patient a harmful idea that was not there before. Freud, the originator and patron saint of psychoanalysis, has answered to the first criticism that a wish whose repression has failed is incomparably stronger when it remain unconscious than when it is made conscious. The unconscious wish cannot be influenced and is not hindered by strivings in the opposite direction, which the conscious wish is inhibited by other conscious wishes of an opposite nature. I shall not take sides on this particular argument, but shall merely content myself with presenting the two points of view, leaving the reader to judge of their merits for himself.

When the unconscious craving is brought to the surface, what becomes of it and what is to be done with it? Partly, say the psychoanalysts, it is "consumed" and overpowered in the very act of bringing it up. Instead of being repressed, it is condemned. The psychoanalyst may also suggest healthy and normal and socially beneficial or harmless ways of gratifying it.

But there is something further. It may, according to Freud, be "sublimated." By sublimation, Freud understands a process which seeks to utilize the sexual energy, immobilized by repressions and set free by analysis, for higher purposes of a non-sexual nature. In other words, the components of the sexual energy can be made to exchange their sexual goal for one more remote and socially valuable. "To the utilization of the energy reclaimed in such a way, in the activities of our mental life, we probably owe the highest cultural achievements. As long as an impulse is repressed, it cannot be sublimated. After the removal of the repression, the way to sublimation is open."

All this is interesting and promising. But alas! The doctrine is violently criticized by many other psychoanalysts. "No normal craving," says one, "can be normally repressed. Nor can it be normally sublimated." And again: "The desirability of sublimation, except as a social convenience, remains to be proved."

In fact, it is doubtful to just what extent Freud himself believed in this theory. In one of his lectures, he said: "If the repression of sexuality is pushed too far it amounts to a robbery committed against the organism." He concluded this lecture with a story. A village community kept a horse which was capable of an enormous amount of work. But the wiseacres thought that it was proving too costly by consuming too much fodder. So they began to cut down its ration, day by day. It finally got so small that the horse was living on one stalk of hay a day, with apparently no ill effects. The next morning he was to be taken to work with no food at all. But on that morning he was found dead in his stall. The "sublimation" of his craving for food had been complete.

The suggestion is plain. Freud is putting the desire for sexual gratification in the same category as the desire for food. I cannot see the justice for that; and I am sorry, if, in pointing out his fallacy, I am obliged to utter a few platitudes. Food is absolutely essential to the life of the individual from the day of birth. There is no one to deny it. Sexuality, however essential to the continuation of the race, has no indispensable connection with the individual. No one has ever been known to live without food. How many have lived without sexual gratification no one can say; but I have no doubt that the number, in its totality, has been amazingly large.

The psychoanalysts point to monks and ordinary individuals who, attempting to deny the flesh, suffered from hallucinations or finally burst forth in abnormal perversions. Most of the examples they cite may be true. All of them may be true. But that would not prove their case. In order to do so, they would have to prove what the logicians call a universal negative. They would have to show that there has never been a case in which the flesh has been denied without physical injury or mental disturbance. Either that, or they would have to supply overwhelming evidence to show that on *a priori* grounds such a thing is impossible. They have not done so. They have not come near doing so. And though it is impossible to prove beyond question of any given individual that he has not indulged in any sexual practice of any kind, yet there is abundant presumptive evidence that thousands of prominent churchmen, scientists, philosophers and quite ordinary individuals have succeeded in absolute chastity and remained otherwise wholly "normal."

And before going any further it would be well to call attention to a point of the highest importance. Altogether apart from the *truth* of one belief or the other, we must consider the *moral effect* of the belief. If you *believe* that you cannot get along without sexual or any other particular gratification, then assuredly you will not be able to. But if you believe that you *can* get along without it, you may have won half the victory. What you *believe* in this respect will have an overwhelming influence upon what you do. If you are convinced that "repression" or "suppression" will lead to mental torture or abnormal outlets, then this fear will be constantly before you. By thinking that you have to yield, you *will* yield. But if you are confident that the desire can be successfully fought, your confidence will vastly increase your strength to fight it. *Whichever your belief, you will tend to make your belief true.* One does not have to be a philosophic pragmatist to appreciate that. I hope I shall be forgiven for a liberal use of italics and repetition on this point; I think they are necessary.

There is another question in regard to this matter. What is a "normal" craving? The psychoanalysts (and perhaps they are not alone in this) apparently put the sexual desire on all fours with the desire for food. But the satisfaction of the desire for food does not result in any reaction. It does not weaken a man. It does not depress. It does not enervate. It does not exhaust. And here we should draw a sharp distinction between two words that up to now I have been using almost interchangeably. I refer to the distinction between a *desire* and a *craving*. We have a *desire* for food, but a *craving* for cigarettes, whiskey, morphine. The first fills a positive need and gives a positive satisfaction. The second is largely negative; it may give a positive satisfaction at the beginning, but in its later stages, especially if one becomes a cigarette or a morphine fiend or a dipsomaniac, it merely relieves a sense of discomfort, agony, or torture, from which one who is not an addict is wholly free.

Is the sexual craving a "normal" craving simply because it is inborn, while a craving for tobacco, alcohol or opium is abnormal because it is acquired? But if this distinction is valid, of what real practical importance is it so far as the individual is concerned? Surely the acquired craving may be fully as intense and overwhelming as the "normal" craving. People who do not believe this may ponder these examples quoted by Dr. Mussey:

> A few years ago a tippler was put into an almshouse in this state (Ohio). Within a few days he had devised various expedients to procure rum but failed. At length, however he hit upon one which was successful. He went into the woodyard of the establishment, placed one hand upon the block and with an axe in the other struck it off at a single blow. With the stump raised and streaming he ran into the house and cried, "Get some rum! Get some rum! My had is off!" In the confusion and bustle of the occasion a bowl of rum was brought, into which he plunged the bleeding member of his body, then raising the bowl to his mouth, drank freely, and exultingly exclaimed, "Now I am satisfied." Dr. J.E. Turner tells of a man who, while under treatment for inebriety, during four weeks secretly drank the alcohol from six jars containing morbid specimens. On asking him why he had committed this loathsome act, he replied: "Sir, it is as impossible for me to control this diseased appetite as it is for me to control the pulsations of my heart."

Do the psychoanalysts, or does anyone else, believe that it is impossible to fight a craving of this sort, and that there is nothing to be done but give in to it? I do not think so. But if a craving of this intensity can be fought, why not the so-called "normal" craving? What would the psychoanalysts consider a "normal outlet" for a "normal" craving? Just how frequent would indulgence in a given "normal" appetite have to be in order to be a "normal outlet"? Will the psychoanalysts, or anyone else, deny that indulgence in itself develops and increases a craving? Surely the psychoanalysts are the first to declare that abnormal perversions of the sexual instinct are acquired, that they began and developed because the sexual instinct originally took a wrong turn, and were intensified because that was persisted in. But when one has admitted all this, one has come rather close to admitting the unquestionable truth that the sexual craving, as it appears in the adult human being, is itself, in the intensity and particular form it takes, very largely an "acquired" craving.

Let us grant the psychoanalysts' contention that an attempt to fight the sexual craving, as it has become developed, may involve mental anxiety, and even, if the craving be powerful enough, mental torture for a time. Would not the struggle against the craving for drink, developed to the intensity in the dipsomaniacs just cited, or even in far less intensity, also involve mental anxiety and torture? Any conquest or act of will worth while involves that. If there were no price attached to will-power, it could be had for the asking.

One last argument may be urged in support of the "normality" of the sexual desire as opposed to other cravings. It may be alleged that, while in its developed and actual adult form, the sexual passion is largely or partly an acquired one (its form and intensity depending to a great extend upon early environment, imitation, decisions at critical times, frequency of indulgence, yet the organism is endowed with an instinctive propensity without which the sexual craving as developed would never have come into existence. This is true. I have not denied it. But if it is true of the sexual desire, it is true of every other desire. It is true of the developed craving for rum, for opium, for morphine, for overindulgence in cigarettes or even in candy, or for mere gluttony. The formation of these cravings is possible because the organism has certain instinctive propensities. Men do not usually form passions for ink-drinking, or for molten lead, or for eating gravel, because the organism has no instinctive propensity for these things. Every desire whatever, no matter how perverted or injurious, is the finished product made from the raw materials of instinctive propensities. There are no other finished products, because there are no other raw materials to make them with.

Reduced to its lowest terms, stripped of its scientific pretensions and its pseudo-scientific trappings and terminology, boiled down from a ponderous literature into a single sentence, the contention of the psychoanalysts was long ago expressed in the epigram of Oscar Wilde: "The only way to get rid of a temptation is to yield to it."

It would be unfair to intimate that this epigram accounted for Oscar Wilde's own private character and sexual practice, and I will not do so. If he thought of his private character at all when he penned it, the epigram may possibly have been considered by him as a justification of his course; but this would not mean that it was a cause. The ethical philosophy of most men is a system of apologetics; it is a result of their own conduct rather than a cause and determinant of it. But all these considerations aside. Let us judge the epigram on its intrinsic merits.

Like all good epigrams, it is at least true in a special sense. And the sense in which the epigram is true is that if you yield to a temptation, you will get rid of it *for the moment*. That is all the truth there is in it. For the very fact that you have yielded to the temptation will make it return at a later time with increased power and urgency. Every time you yield to it, you do two things; you increase the intensity of the desire and lessen the power of resistance. You form a habit of yielding. You form a habit of yielding not only to that, but to all other cravings—and we have learned what habits are. You develop and strengthen the craving by use, just as you develop a muscle by use. The parallel is exact. In exercising your muscles, you temporarily fatigue them and wear them down. But this very breaking down of tissues calls nutrition into the worn muscles, and when the fatigue is past, and the processes of repair have been completed, the muscles are all the harder and stronger.

On the other hand, every time you resist a desire you strengthen your power to resist. Every desire grows by gratification. Feed the desire, it will fatten and grow great; starve it, it will greatly weaken. It may even die of inanition. This is the true application of Freud's story of the horse. The common experience, not of neurotics and paranoiacs, but of mankind in general, proves this over and over again. It does not need laboratory experiments or elaborate psychiatry to demonstrate it.

It ought not be necessary, but to shield my remarks from misconstruction and misrepresentation, I want to defend myself against any taint of Puritanism in the invidious sense in which the psychoanalysts and Mr. H.L. Mencken use that word. I do not denounce the sexual act as immoral in itself. I do not declaim against the gratification of the sexual passions in what the psychoanalysts call a "normal married life," provided that gratification is continent, and does not reach the point where it undermines or endangers physical and nervous and mental health and well-being. But I do contend that if, through economic or other circumstances, or disinclination, or inability to fall in love, a man either does not marry or delays marriage, it is perfectly possible for him to lead an absolutely chaste and normal life; and of two unmarried men having equal sexual propensities to begin with the man who voluntarily restrains them the more is the stronger and the better character.

I am merely making this one point; that the sexual craving can be fought, that it can be lived down, that it can be conquered, and that the conquest of it would immensely strengthen the character, and make most other moral victories comparatively easy. I hold to the ideal of Huxley, of a man "who, no stunted ascetic, is full of life and fire, but whose passions are trained to come to heel by a vigorous will, the servant of a tender conscience."

Perhaps there are psychoanalysts who will agree with all this. Perhaps there are psychoanalysts who will protest against my fulminations, saying they do not hold the views I attribute to them, that I either do not understand their views or that I willfully distort them. If I have been unfair, if I have through lack of discrimination blamed all psychoanalysts for the faults of a few, if I have unjustly damned the leaders for the views disseminated by ardent but muddle-headed and ignorant disciples, I am sorry. I have meant only to assault a particular idea. I have tried to be fair; and wherever possible I have taken the psychoanalysts own words to state their position. But whatever the psychoanalysts do or do not teach, there is no doubt at all about the popular impression of what they teach, and the popular impression (which is the all-important thing) is that they believe it not only impossible to conquer the sexual passion, but highly dangerous to try.

The vicious doctrine existed long before the psychoanalysts, but the present menace is that psychoanalysis may foster and encourage it, by seeming to lend it scientific foundation and support. The doctrine must be utterly demolished, and everything that appears to offer it respect worthy standing must be examined and exposed. This is all I have attempted to do.

XII
CONCENTRATION

THUS far I have spoken of the breaking and forming of habits, and of the acquisition of will-power; but for the most part I have given only scattered hints on what to do with your will-power after you have it. Most of these hints have been negative; they have talked of the avoidance of certain acts; and where they have been positive, where they have talked of the performance of acts, they have been altogether lofty and abstract. We have now to descend from the empyrean of generalities to the forest of details.

Your ultimate ends and yearning I shall, for the moment, take for granted. I assume that you know what you want, that you have definite ideas on where the treasure of happiness is buried, and that you merely seek aid in securing the implements to dig for it. Your aim in life may be wealth, power, fame, or a partnership in the lime and cement business. Assuming its existence, whatever it may be, and the willingness also to pay the price for it, we have now to inquire how the price is to be paid.

Your effort of will is not thrown out all at once. You are not asked to pay cash down in full. You are permitted—nay, you are obliged—to pay for your end in installments, in relatively small efforts of will. But these efforts of will must be continuous and sustained. If you miss a payment, the penalty imposed will be exorbitant, and you will have to make a much greater total payment in the end. On the other hand, if your payments are made promptly, you will find the amount called for diminishing all the time.

With most ends, one of the requisites will be the acquisition of knowledge—whether one's ultimate purpose be material success or the pure search for Truth. The acquisition of this knowledge will require thought and study, and thought and study will require concentration.

Now this concentration will be mainly of two kinds—what I shall call minute-to-minute concentration, and what I shall call night-after-night concentration. Minute-to-minute concentration is the ability to keep your mind upon a certain subject for a given period, say for ten minutes, one half hour or two hours without interruption. Night-after-night concentration is the ability to specialize in a certain subject or in a certain branch of that subject until you have mastered it thoroughly, before advancing to other subjects.

Ere I go further I may have to justify the consideration of this question by asserting that concentration is primarily an act of will. It need not necessarily be so, any more than any other good or noble or success-forwarding act need be an act of will. If you enjoy working, getting up early, remaining home nights, staying sober, you will do so without effort. If you are interested in a book or in a particular subject, you will read it or meditate upon it without effort. But you need will-power in action precisely because you do not enjoy doing these commendable things, and you need will-power in reading, thought or writing precisely because your mind will otherwise be distracted by lack or lapses of interest in the subject at hand or by greater interest in something else.

Now when you take up the sublime task of training the mind to concentrate, you must remember that the act of will involved is the same in principle as any other act of will. Before you begin, you must be certain in your own mind that the end is worth while. There is a price attached to concentration, as there is to anything of value. Concentration is not a beautifully abstract quality of mind. We cannot concentrate in general. The very word concentration implies specialization; it means concentrating on some particular thing, and when we devote all or most of our time and attention to one particular subject, we must necessarily have less time for other subjects. In other words, we must be content to remain somewhat ignorant of them, at least for a time.

This applies particularly to night-after-night concentration. If you devote one evening's study to the quantity theory of money, the next evening to the problem of the freedom of the will, the next to incidents in the life of Theodore Roosevelt, the next to historic types of lampshades, your mind may eventually become an interesting depository of stray bits of knowledge, arousing the same sort of quaint enjoyment in the minds of your associates as an old curiosity shop, or a second-hand bookstore in which yellow-backed novels of passion and intrigue rub shoulders with scientific treatises and religious sermons.

But such miscellaneous reading is not helping you in any ultimate purpose. You are getting nowhere. You will become neither an economist, nor an ethicist, nor a man versed in biography, nor anything else describable with a complimentary name. By trying to know something about everything, you will not only miss knowing everything about something, but you may miss really knowing anything about anything. Your mind my miss the one advantage of an old curiosity shop—that the pieces of furniture in it, though they may not match each other, are at least in themselves complete. If you give only one or two evenings to a subject, your knowledge of it may be as useless as a chair with two legs. But if you are willing to realize that any useful knowledge whatever requires specialization, that it means keeping evening after evening on the same subject; if you take pride in really knowing something about something, then you will be willing to remain ignorant of certain subjects, at least for a given time. Even if, like Bacon, you take all human knowledge as your province, you must remember that even a traveler who circles the globe can go to only one place at one time.

I have spoken here only of keeping to one subject on those evenings on which you do choose to study. I have not spoken of the evenings given to other things. It may not be advisable to give six or seven evenings a week to study. One needs one's play to keep from going stale. But there are limits even to this principle. No man will become an Aristotle or a Dun Scotus on an evening a week. "Most careers," remarked a newspaper writer recently, "are made or marred in the hours after supper."

What applies to night-after-night concentration applies with much greater force to minute-to-minute concentration. If the mind is ever to accomplish anything useful, it must be able to keep itself for a reasonable time on a given subject. The very completion of a train of thought on any subject whatsoever depends upon it. And the rules are the same old rules. You must first be fully certain in your own mind that the end is worthwhile. For when you are upon any given train of thought, you will find new paths opening up on either side, pleasant paths, paths that seem to led to worthwhile destinations, paths you are tempted to explore. But you must force yourself to keep on the road that you began. You must first get to the end of that. You may make mental note of these potential digressions, to return to them at some later time; or if you fear you are going to forget them, you may make written note of them as they suggest themselves.

Concentration is not a virtue in itself. The value of concentration depends entirely on the value of the subject concentration depends entirely on the value of the subject concentrated upon. The only qualification to this remark is that it may often be better really to concentrate upon a less important subject that to play and dabble with a more important one; for the less important subject, if concentrated upon, will at least be mastered.

I have dealt with this subject of concentration rather extensively in a former book, *Thinking as a Science*. It was there treated mainly from the standpoint of the intellect; here it must be treated from the standpoint of the will; but as the two cannot really be kept separate, and as I would only be likely to repeat myself anyway, I take the liberty of doing so openly:

> Much of our mind wandering is due to the fact that we are not fully convinced of the importance of the problem being attacked or that we regard other problems or ideas as more important. Concentration consists in devoting one's mind to the solution of one problem. During our train of thought associations bring up new ideas or suggest problems which do not bear on the question at hand. Now when we wander, when we follow up these irrelevant ideas or suggested problems, or when we happen to glance at something or hear something and begin to think of that, we do so because of a half-conscious belief that the new idea, problem or fact needs attending to is important. I have already pointed out that if this new idea is important it will be so only by accident. If we were consciously to ask ourselves whether any of these irrelevant problems were as important as the one we were concentrating upon or even important at all, we should find, nine times out of ten, that they were not.

Mind-wandering is only a habit. It must be broken just like other bad habits. "But," I hear you say, "all this is beyond my control. I can't keep my mind on a book when somebody insists on talking in the same room. I can't write anything when the family in the apartment upstairs plays the victrola. I can't keep myself to a train of thought with constant interruptions!"

But, with all due respect to you and with full realization of the risk I run of losing *your* respect, I insist that you can. You have done it. Certain allowances must always be made for the unspeakable noises that other people make, but you can ignore them easily enough when the time comes. Can you not recall, when as a boy you read the adventures of Jack Harkaway and the Chinamen, so that you became unconscious of the very room in which you were sitting? Has the memory of the smile given you by a certain wonderful girl never come between you and a very prosaic ledger, obliterating the figures as completely as if they were the fancy and the smile of reality? Has your wife never had to ask you a question two or three times at dinner before you answered, simply because you were completely wrapped up in some thought of a business unpleasantry that day, and did not know that she had spoken? All these forms of involuntary concentration, of which you were not conscious, were possible because the interest in the subject was intense enough.

Poverty in freshness of idea and in varied expressions tempts me again to quote from myself:

> Whenever a person is left alone for a short time, with no one to talk to and no "reading matter"; when for instance, he is standing at a station waiting for his train, or sitting at a restaurant table waiting for his order, or hanging on a subway strap when he has forgotten to buy a newspaper, his "thoughts" tend to run along the tracks they have habitually taken. If a young man usually allows a popular tune to float through his head, that will be most likely to

happen; if he usually thinks of that young lady, he will most likely think of her then; if he has often imagined himself as some great political orator making a speech amid the plaudits of the multitude, he is likely to see a mental picture of himself swinging his arms, waving flags and gulping water.

The only way a man can put a stop to such pleasant but uneducative roamings, is to snap off his train of daydreaming the first moment he becomes aware of it, and to address his mind to some useful serious subject. His thoughts will be almost sure to leak away again. They may do this as often as fifteen times in half an hour. But the second he becomes aware of it, he should dam up the stream and send his thoughts along the channel he has laid out for them. If he has never done this, he will find the effort great. But if he merely resolves now that the next time his mind wanders he shall stop it in this manner, his resolve will tend to make itself felt. If he succeeds in following this practice once, it will be much easier a second time. Every time he does this it will become increasingly easy, until he will have arrived at the point where his control over his thoughts will be almost absolute. Not only will it be increasingly easy for him to turn his mind to serious subjects. It will become constantly more pleasurable. Frivolous and petty trains of thought will become more and more intolerable.

XIII
A PROGRAM OF WORK

MOST of us live in the Street of By-and-By. We honestly intend to do certain things, and for some strange reason we keep on intending to do them. There is nothing specially difficult about them. They demand no gritting of teeth, no heroic sacrifice. They are simply not as pleasant as certain other things. They do not have to be done until a certain time, or perhaps there is no particular time at all at which they have to be done. They can be done just as well tomorrow as today. So we put them off till tomorrow—that tragic tomorrow that never comes. We become members of what one writer has called the "Going To" family. We enlist in the Army of the Procrastinators.

The worst of it is, that many of us do not look upon the doing of these numberless small tasks as anything requiring will-power at all, simply because they do not come in the teeth-gritting class. We intend to do them, and we are apt to think that our intention of doing them makes them as good as done. We are like the habitual cigarette smoker who tells you he could quit at any time—the thing has no hold on him—only he doesn't want to quit. When we find that many of these little tasks are going by default, many of us, instead of blaming ourselves indulge in a great deal of self-pity at our lack of time. But a few of us catch glimpses of the truth; we suspect that we are not as efficient as we might be; we may even suspect that our procrastination has something to do with lack of will-power. These two suspicions are correct.

Aside from any moral benefit, it would be an untold blessing in itself if we could get these things done—if we had, for instance, a private secretary who would work for the mere honor of it and would not have even to receive instructions. I refer to such tasks as writing personal letters to friends; working off letters that you "owe" to people; paying bills; sending in your coupons to collect interest on a bond; taking a pairs of shoes around to be half-soled, or calling for a pair you left there; sorting out the old papers in your desk; bringing neatness out of chaos. ... I need not elaborate further. You have probably been already reminded unpleasantly of some concrete tasks.

These tasks are not performed by intentions to perform them. The first requisite is to set a definite time for them, and to allow nothing to make you postpone that time. Instead of saying, "I will have to write Fred; I really must write Fred; it's a shame how long I've been putting it off," you will say, "I will write Fred next Tuesday," or I will write to Fred no later than next Tuesday." And you will keep a desk calendar or some other form of reminder, and your promise to yourself you will regard as sacred.

Now it may not make a great deal of difference to Fred whether he gets your letter next Tuesday or whether he does not get it until two weeks from next Tuesday. But it will make a great deal of difference to you. You will be disciplining yourself morally. You will be building up a will. Beware of curling your lip because these tasks are individually insignificant. The most imposing edifices that humanity has constructed (if I must be eloquent) have been built only by little brick on little brick. Moreover, you will find that these little tasks are getting themselves done. You will live a completer life, free from the ever-present preoccupation of tasks unfinished. And you will experience the peculiarly delightful gratification that comes from a sense of efficiency.

Note that there is nothing rigid or brittle about such a program. You may not want to write Fred immediately after you get his letter, for you may not want the correspondence to be too frequent. But by marking a certain definite time you can do what you had not previously done.

A program of work may be laid out for the year, for the week, for the day or for the hour; or one program may be contained within the other. You should lay out your longest range program first, for that will define the direction and scope of your efforts. The nature of this long program will depend upon your ultimate purposes in life. Your aim may simply be general culture, but even in this instance you will realize that haphazard reading is of little value, and you will draw up a list of books to be "covered" that year. Or you may decide that specialization would be more beneficial, and you may say to yourself: "for the following year I will devote my evenings to the study of money and banking," or you may decide to make it the history of English literature, or the appreciation of painting and a critical knowledge of the great masters.

Having thus defined your efforts for the year, so that you know exactly the goal to which you are heading, you may come directly to a plan for the week. You may decide that two or three hours should be given to your study or improvement on Monday, Tuesday, Thursday and Friday evenings; or you may, if you think you have the will-power, allow for something "turning up" on one of those nights, and simply set aside any four evenings a week. I insert the phrase "if you think you have the will-power" because this more elastic plan does, paradoxically, require more will-power than the more rigid program. On Monday and Tuesday something is likely to turn up—you may be tempted to go to a moving picture, some friend may suggest bridge—and knowing that your program does not tie you down to Monday or Tuesday, you may accede; but you will find yourself paying for it heavily at the end of the week; and four evenings in succession, especially if they include Saturday evening, may strain your will-power to the breaking point. Moreover, in making engagements ahead you are likely to over-commit yourself.

"I suppose I could learn it just as well at home as by going to night-school," you have often heard people say, "but I find that I can't study at home." Here is proof that home-study requires more will-power than going to night-school; yet night-school is far more rigid, both in its evenings a week and in its hours during those evenings, than home-study could possibly be. It is precisely because of this rigidity that night-school is easier to attend.

But a further element must also be admitted. It is much easier to say to a friend: " I'm sorry' I'd like to go. But I have to go to night-school," than it is to say, "I'm sorry; but I have to—stay home and study." Your friend is likely to be skeptical. For some reason he may be unable to see that an obligation to yourself is quite as sacred as an obligation to others. And once he finds that your program is elastic, your case is doomed. Study, if you must, on evenings when others would like to have you go out, but not when he would. This is his attitude; and it is going to take all your resources of tact to meet it. Moreover, the truth must be told; we are ashamed of having our friends discover that we are seeking self-improvement. That is why we shrink for confessing our real reasons.

Your first tendency, doubtless, especially in drawing up any program of work or of little things to do in a single night, will be to plan too much. You will find yourself greatly underestimating the time it takes you to perform a particular task, or greatly overestimating the number of tasks you can perform. A program is valuable if for no other reason than that it brings out, as nothing else could, how you have been frittering away your time before you started to formulate programs. Even if you do not live up to your schedule, you will probably get more work done than you would have without one. But it is bad policy habitually to over plan. You may arrive at the point where you will not even *expect* to live up to your scheme. It is much easier for the discipline of will-power to plan modestly and to carry out your schedule than to plan greatly and fail. The first builds self-confidence; the second destroys it.

XIV
THE DAILY CHALLENGE

WILL-POWER in its highest sense, is associated with the Napoleons, the Robert Bruces, and the Luthers. We connect it either with great historic characters, men of action who have shaken the world, or with the noble and almost incredible sacrifices of the Christian martyrs.

Will-power in the heroic sense is not dead. If any one had ever thought so, he must have stopped believing so in 1914. Millions of men went forth to die for their faith and seven million dead on the battlefield are seven million crushing answers to the cynic. If men will show such will for their country, they will show even more for their religious faith. Lest we forget the sacrifices of a former age, let me quote a few extracts from Taine's account, taken from Noailles, Fox, Neal and other sources:

> In three years, under Mary, nearly three hundred persons, men, women, old and young, some all but children, allowed themselves to be burned alive rather than abjure. . . . "No one will be crowned," said one of them, "but they who fight like men; and he who endures to the end shall be saved." Doctor Rogers was burned first, in presence of his wife and ten children, one at the breast. He had not been told before hand, and was sleeping soundly. The wife of the keeper of Newgate woke him, and told him that he must burn that day. "Then," said he, "I need not truss my points." In the midst of the flames he did not seem to suffer. "His children stood by consoling him, in such a way that he looked as if they were conducting him to a merry marriage." . . . Thomas

Tomkins, a weaver of Shoreditch, being asked by Bishop Bonner if he could stand the fire well, bade him to try it. "Bonner took Tompkins by the fingers, and held his hand directly over the flame," to terrify him. But "he never shrank, till the veins and the sinews burst, and the water (blood) did spirt in Mr. Harpsfield's face." Bishop Hooper was burned three times over in a small fire of green wood. There was too little wood and the wind turned aside the smoke. He cried out, "For God's love, good people, let me have more fire." His legs and thighs were roasted; one of his hands fell off before he expired; he endured this three-quarters of an hour; before him in a box was his pardon, on condition that he would retract.

Such examples with all their horror, are a mighty inspiration. They are examples of pure will. We do not know what part of the astounding achievements of Napoleon to assign to his will and what part to the intellect which was its servant. The fortitude of these martyrs was a fortitude made possible by the will alone.

But however inspiring may be such examples, we must guard against connecting our conception of will-power too closely with them. If we place our conception of will-power too high, we are in danger of failing to recognize it in its humbler forms. The opportunity seldom comes when the will is put to such a test, or anything remotely approaching such a test.

The writers of the magazine advertisements for the will-power courses conceive a man of will-power as a man who "gets on," an E.H. Harriman or a J.P. Morgan, a dominant personality, who must assume leadership and power; who bends others to his will, or breaks them if they will not bend; who gets to his goal, if need be, over dead bodies, but who gets to his goal. This is an elevating conception, but the average man of talent is apt to find it a trifle unreal and beside the point after he has finished Lesson One that evening and gone to work the next day. He is resolved to mow down all opposition, but when he gets to the office he finds no opposition. Everybody says Good Morning, pleasantly, though a few wonder vaguely why he has set his jaw so tightly. If he is a bookkeeper, he goes to his ledger and finds the same columns of figures to add up, the same elusive discrepancies to straighten out; and you can't use will-power on figures, because they wouldn't understand it. You can only use will-power on persons. But if he is a sales clerk he cannot "dominate" the customers; he must be pleasant and tactful. He might tell the floorwalker what he really thought of him, and that might give satisfaction to the soul, but it would be of doubtful value in getting ahead in business. And even a bank or a railroad president meets day after day the same routine problems, many of which involve heavy responsibility, shrewd and mature judgment, and sometimes a good deal of thought, but hardly will-power.

The need for will-power thus seems a distant need, which arises perhaps one day in a hundred, or one in a thousand. In fact, some people seem to feel that there are no outlets for will-power in this workaday world, unless you go out of your way to create them. This appears to be the opinion of no less a thinker than William James, who writes in his *Psychology:*

> Keep the faculty of effort alive in you by a little gratuitous exercise every day. That is, be systematically ascetic or heroic in little unnecessary points, do every day or two something for no other reason than that you would rather not do it, so that when the hour of dire need draws nigh, it may find you not unnerved and untrained to stand the test. Asceticism of this sort is like the insurance which a man pays on his house and goods. The tax does him no

good at the time and possibly never brings a return. But if the fire *does* come, his having paid it will be his salvation from ruin. So with the man who has daily inured himself to habits of concentration attention, energetic volition and self-denial in unnecessary things. He will stand like a tower when everything rocks around him and when his softer fellow-mortals are winnowed like chaff in the blast.

This is a noble passage, but I cannot accept James's implied view that daily life gives so few opportunities for the real exercise of will. Our whole modern journey from the incubator to the crematorium is taken in laps of twenty-four hours each; each divided sharply from the other; each with its routine much like the other; but each with its own challenge. And our way of meeting that challenge from day to day is our way of meeting the whole challenge of life. Every day we are faced with a challenge, sometimes large, often small, but it is always there if we but face it. We do not have to create it. We do not have to do unnecessary things. And if we meet it, we pay a premium for which we receive a return and sometimes a handsome one, whether our house burn down or not.

One test of whether you have met this challenge or not is in the way you feel at the end of the day. If you have met it, you will be rewarded with a glow of soul. If you have evaded or postponed it, your lot will be a sense of guilt. It may be ever so slight, but it will always be there, an uneasiness, like dirt in a corner.

I have already mentioned the little daily duties that most of us put off or leave undone. But there are duties of a more serious sort, duties that require one not only to overcome laziness but to surmount moral fear. Principal among these are unpleasant interviews.

Let us take the very practical matter of asking for a raise. You think you are worth more money. You know you are. You have always known it. You have been waiting long enough for the boss to find it out, but the boss has proved either singularly stupid or singularly selfish, and you have determined either to enlighten him or to uplift him spiritually. Your mind is fully made up.

But though your mind was made up a week ago, you haven't asked him yet because on one day you had a mountain of work that had to be shoveled out of the way, and on the next you had been out late the night before and didn't feel equal to an interview, and on the next you didn't look very neat and on the next you were waiting for some mistake to blow over and on the next the boss wasn't in a good mood. In fact, you will tell yourself anything except that you didn't have the courage.

And yet to put off such an interview, when you have fully determined that it must be had, is like putting off getting up in the morning, or putting off diving into cold water when you have gone down for a swim. The longer you stand on the diving board, the colder the water seems to get, the more terrifying becomes the height at which you are standing from it. There is a psychological theory that emotion follows action and not action emotion; that you do not run away from a bear because a fear seizes you, but that fear seizes you because you are running away. Whatever of truth there may be in this, it is certainly true that though you may hesitate; and the like applies to interviewing the boss for an increase.

Here again I do not suggest inflexibility. It is sometimes better to do a certain thing in the future; but if you really mean to do it at all, I insist upon fixing a definite time.

Another challenge which is apt to occur once or twice on almost any day is the necessity for pronouncing that most difficult of all words for the tongue—No. A friend who has drifted from one job to another, finally becomes a salesman for oil stock, and wants you to "invest" in it; another wants to borrow money; another wants you to go into partnership with him; another wants you to spend with him an evening that you have set aside for study; another offers you a drink after you have signed the pledge. When you are with a young lady, a professional beggar, whom you privately suspect to be a fraud, an idler and a parasite, perhaps better off than you are, asks you for just a little silver change.

The answer you would like to give in each case is No. Yet you fear to give offense; you fear to jeopardize your friendship; you fear a nasty retort; you fear having to defend your position; you fear embarrassment. Often by refusing without unkindness, but with firmness and candor and tact, you can reduce giving offense to a minimum, but it is idle to imagine that you can altogether avoid it. That part which is altogether unavoidable must be faced courageously. A man cannot respect himself if he grants a request or gives money to a beggar not because he believes the request is fair, or to relieve the beggar's distress, but simply because he cannot look his supplicant in the eye and tell him No. And the necessity for saying No is a daily necessity, an unpleasant duty that you do not have to go out of your way to find.

To add to all this, as a daily exercise for will-power, there is always the infinitude of bad habits to be broken and of good habits to be formed. As a mere specific example, a cold shower every morning, if you are physically fitted for it, is an excellent will exercise, which more than pays for itself in its effects upon your health.

XV
SECOND AND THIRD WINDS

WE have dealt with the humbler tasks. We come now to the tasks that are not so humble. We have considered how we may perform our routine duties. But men of a higher stamp, men with an aim in life, men who want to mean something, are not satisfied with merely performing routine duties. They aspire to something nobler and more soul-stirring. Not content with fulfilling the duties the world lays upon them, they want to lay upon themselves duties to fulfill. Perhaps, with Bernard Shaw, they feel that the true joy in life is

> the being used for a purpose recognized by yourself as a mighty one; the being thoroughly worn out before you are thrown on the scrap-heap; the being a force of Nature instead of a feverish, selfish little clod of ailments and grievances, complaining that the world will not devote itself to making you happy.

An ideal like that in itself will exalt a man, and give part of the strength needed for its own realization. But it carries with it a great danger. This is the danger that the ideal, instead of finding its outlet in action may evaporate into day-dreams and gorgeous intentions whose date for fulfillment is always set at some vague time in the future. As a preliminary antidote for such a danger, I suggest these lines of Goethe:

> Lose this day loitering—'twill be the same story
> Tomorrow—and the next more dilatory.
> Then indecision brings its own delays.

> And days are lost lamenting over days.
> Are you in earnest? Seize this very minute—
> What you can do, or dream you can, begin it.
> Courage has genius, power and magic in it;
> Only engage, and then the mind grows heated—
> Begin it and the work will be completed.

What Goethe saw so powerfully, William James saw later, and elaborated the idea in a theory which goes beyond even this. That theory appeared in an essay called "The Energies of Men." In all English and American literature there is nothing of its short length—a mere thirty-five pages—so calculated to inspire a man with a passion for work. It is published in his *Memories and Studies* (Longmans, Green), and separately. By all means read it. Read it, if you can, before your next meal. If it does not inspire you with a passion to go out immediately and do something large and glorious, you are probably not normal.

Every sentence and illustration of that essay is so indispensable and full of meaning, that I cannot hope to give you any summary, or the "gist" of it. I can, however, give you a premonition of what it is about, and this itself can best be done, for the most part, in James's own words:

> Everyone knows what it is to start a piece of work, either intellectual or muscular, feeling stale. And everybody knows what it is to 'warm up' to his job. The process of warming up gets particularly striking in the phenomenon known as 'second wind.' On usual occasions we make a practice of stopping an occupation as soon as we meet the first effective layer (so to call it) of fatigue. We have then walked, played, or worked 'enough,' so we desist. That amount of fatigue is an effacious obstruction on this side of which our usual life is cast. But if an unusual necessity

forces us to press onward, a surprising thing occurs. The fatigue gets worse up to a certain critical point, when gradually or suddenly it passes away, and we are fresher than before. We have evidently tapped a level of new energy, masked until then by the fatigue-obstacle usually obeyed. There may be a layer after layer of this experience. A third and fourth 'wind' may supervene. Mental activity shows the phenomenon as well as physical, and in exceptional cases we may find beyond the very extremity of fatigue-distress, amounts of ease and power that we never dreamed ourselves to own—sources of strength habitually not taxed at all because habitually we never push through the obstruction never pass those early critical points.

For many years James mused upon the phenomenon of second wind, trying to find a physiological theory. It is evident, he decided, that our organism has

> stored-up reserves of energy that are ordinarily not called upon, but that may be called upon; deeper and deeper strata of combustible or explosible material . . . repairing themselves by rest as well as do the superficial strata.

He compares our energy-budge to our nutritive budget.

> Physiologists say that a man is in "nutritive equilibrium" when day after day he neither gains nor loses weight. But the odd thing is that this condition may obtain on astonishingly different amount of food. Take a man in nutritive equilibrium, and systematically increases or lessen his rations. In the first case he will begin to gain weight, in the second case to lose it. The change will be greatest on the first day, less on the second, still less on the third; and so on, till he has gained all that he will gain, or lost all that he will lose on that altered diet. He is now

in nutritive equilibrium again, but with a new weight; and this neither lessens nor increases because his various combustion-processes have adjusted themselves to the changed dietary....

Just so one can be in what I might call "efficiency-equilibrium" (neither gaining nor losing power when once the equilibrium is reached) on astonishingly different quantities of work, no matter in what direction the work may be measured. It may be physical work, intellectual work, moral work or spiritual work.

"Of course," he admits, "there are limits: the trees don't grow into the sky.... But the very same individual, pushing his energies to their extreme, may in a vast number of cases keep the pace up day after day, and find no 'reaction' of a bad sort, so long as decent hygienic conditions are preserved."

These are astonishing statements; approaching if true, a veritable revelation. But James goes on to illustrate the truth of his statement on a wholesale scale:

Country people and city people, as a class, illustrate this difference. The rapid rate of life, the number of decisions in an hour, the many things to keep account of, in a busy city man's or woman's life, seem monstrous to a country brother. He doesn't see how we live at all. A day in New York or Chicago fills him with terror. The danger and noise make it appear like a permanent earth quake. But *settle* him there, and in a year or two he will have caught the pulse-beat. He will vibrate to the city's rhythms; and if he only succeeds in his avocation, whatever that may be, he will find a joy in all the hurry and the tension, he will keep the pace as well as any of us, and get as much out of himself in any week as he ever did in ten weeks in the country...

> The transformation, moreover, is a chronic one: the new level of energy becomes permanent.

How are we to produce these marvelous results? How are we to draw on our vast unused powers and make them available? How are we to keep ourselves going at the highest efficient speed on all six cylinders, instead of idling along, knocking on one, losing compression on another, and missing on three?

In the instance of the country folk in the city, the stimuli of those who successfully respond and undergo the transformation, are, in James's words, "the example of others, and crowd-pressure and contagion." There is also duty. "The duties of new offices of trust are constantly producing this effect on the human beings appointed to them."

But there are other stimuli than these for bringing out our latent resources. I cannot quote all the inspiring examples which James cites to show the diverse ways in which the resources have been drawn on, but I can summarize the "stimuli" which he credits for them. They include, in addition to those just mentioned; excitements, ideas, efforts, love, anger, religious crises, love-crises, indignation-crises, despair in some cases, the suppression of "fear thought" which is the "self-suggestion of inferiority" (phrases he borrows from Horace Fletcher), systematic asceticism, "beginning with easy tasks, passing to harder ones, and exercising day by day."

Finally he adds:

> The normal opener of deeper and deeper levels of energy is the will. The difficulty is to use it, to make the effort which the word "volition" implies. ... It is notorious that a single successful effort of moral volition, such as saying "no" to some habitual temptation, or performing some courageous act, will launch a man on a higher level of

energy for days and weeks, will give him a new range of power. "In the act of uncorking the whisky bottle which I had brought home to get drunk upon." Said a man to me, "I suddenly found myself running out into the garden, where I smashed it on the ground. I felt so happy and uplifted after this act, that for two months I wasn't tempted to touch a drop."

There is one stimulus to breaking down the fatigue-barriers which James, though he occasionally appears to get close to it, does not mention. It is a very important stimulus. In fact, I am quite prepared to call it the most important of them all. It is sometimes derivative; and includes in art one or two of the stimuli already referred to. This stimulus is *intensity of interest*.

Interest, excitement, absorption in the pursuit of an object, make you forget yourself and your discomforts. A man who is so tired out from the day at the office that he cannot read his newspaper on the subway, who brings home some work and is too tired to understand it after dinner, though he makes several attempts and several fresh starts to "get his mind down to it," may none the less turn to a detective story, and follow the course of its characters, the clues, the shrewd mental workings of the detective, trying to anticipate his deductions and conclusions, all with the most intense concentration and the highest relish. He may feel too worn out mentally to sit home and read a consular report on a matter of interest to his business, a report containing no long chains of reasoning nor a single subtle statement; yet he will not feel too tired to dress for the theatre and enjoy a Shaw comedy to the full, with one clever and subtle epigram touching off another like a package of firecrackers. A stupid office boy will show intelligence about baseball and professional boxing gossip. The explanation in each case is simply a difference in interest.

This principle in the mental field applies quite as strongly in the physical. A man who would be completely tired out if he beat a rug for his wife, will play five sets of tennis of an afternoon, absorbing ten times as much physical energy. The first is "work," the second "play." Every soldier is familiar with the immense difference it makes to him whether he is drilling with or without music; in the first case his step is lighter, his heart is lighter, his rifle is lighter; his fatigue is half gone. Modern gymnasiums are beginning to recognize this effect by giving their callisthenic exercises to music of a piano or a phonograph. But both drilling and calisthenics are considered "work" and the principle is still better illustrated at a dance, where a man is quite unconscious (unless his partner is awkward or unattractive) that he is working. Every man who has ever adventured upon a ballroom floor can tell you how much better he can dance, how much more uncontrollable is his craving to dance, how much longer he can dance, with good music than with bad. A man will go to a social affair, and he will dance and dance; he will be there for every encore; he will clap and clap for more; and when the affair is over and the stains of "Home, Sweet Home" have sent him home in spite of himself, he will fall into a taxicab in a state of utter collapse; and when he is arrived home, will scarcely have the energy to undress for bed. He will finally be in bed at anywhere from half past one to half past three in the morning. But let him stay in the office till after midnight, let him "work" till half past one or half past three in the morning, and till the end of his life he will never have done telling about that prodigy of accomplishment.

The same principle which applies to the common man applies to the genius. It may sometimes even appear to make a common man into a genius. The histories of philosophy and science abound with examples of thinkers apparently apathetic and indolent by nature, but who, once upon the scent of a new and original theory or discovery, have bent themselves to an enormous and astounding amount of thinking and reading and experimenting and fact-collecting. The infinite patience and industry of Darwin once he had hit upon the idea of biological evolution and the struggle for survival, and the change of Herbert Spencer from indolence to ambition, once he had glimpsed evolution as a universal law, applying not only to the body, but to the mind, to nations, to social and economic institutions, to language, to the stars, to morals, to manners, to beliefs and theories, and the marvelous erudition which he acquired in gathering all these facts and weaving them into a gigantic system of twenty volumes of philosophy in spite of the grave handicaps of poor finances and poor health—these are but two examples out of hundreds that might be cited.

The common idea that geniuses as a rule are lazy, with a distinct aversion for work in general is one of the greatest of untruths. The untruth has its origin in the fact that geniuses usually have an aversion toward the particular kind of work which their fathers or the world would set them to. The father would set the son up in some respectable profession, make him a minister, a lawyer, a stockbroker, or have him succeed the father as head of the tin-plate mills; but the genius will have none of it. He is neither docile nor tractable; he will forge his own path. But, if he be a true genius, then once he has struck that path, which natural inclination, nay, which every fiber of his being demands that he follow, his industry and pertinacity will make that of your average respectable business man look like the merest dawdling. If Goethe had been lazy, could he have turned out sixty volumes? Could

Defoe have turned out two hundred and ten? Could Shakespeare, greatest of them all, have turned out thirty-seven plays and acted in them? Take any classic writer of fiction, Scott or Dickens or Dumas or Dostoevsky, and recall what an imposing thing is the "complete works" of any one of them when gathered in uniform binding. Could indolent men have wrought these things?

We may consider even the classic examples of literary indolence—Samuel Johnson, let us say. He usually wrote only when spurred on by the need of money, and then only enough to keep himself and his wife from starving. After he was pensioned by the king, he indulged his natural sloth by lying in bed until mid-day and after. Yet he carried on his magazine, the *Rambler*, twice-a-week for two years single-handed; he produced eight volumes of essays, many volumes of biographies and his immense Dictionary; and to pay for his mother's funeral wrote *Rasselas* in eight nights. It is evident that when Johnson once set to a task, his powers of sustained concentration were such as only the rarest mortals can equal.

What we find in literature, we find in every other art. A lazy Michael Angelo could not have built St. Peters, to say nothing of his other works. A lazy Beethoven or Mozart could not have composed the number of works that these men did. Franz Schubert, known for his easy-going Bohemian life, always out of funds, always care free, yet managed to turn out several overtures, eight symphonies, and six hundred songs!

The catalog does not end with literature and the arts. Napoleon was such a gourmand for work that he could frequently spare only four hours a night for sleep, and sometimes went without that. Thomas A. Edison is perhaps the greatest inventor that the world has ever seen. By either inventing or improving the electric light, the phonograph, the telephone, the moving picture, and patenting hundreds of other inventions, he has done more that any single man to make our present-day material civilization what it is. Yet though now in his seventies, he hardly ever takes a holiday, sleeps only four consecutive hours and works at all hours of the day and night. One could go on and on.

And how are these prodigious achievements possible? Geniuses and artists do not doggedly drag themselves through their work. That is not their attitude toward it. They get so much work done because the work they do is their play, their recreation, their passion.

And it is so because of their intensity of interest. "Warming up to one's work," as cited by James, and the manner in which "the mind grows heated," as expressed by Goethe, are simply ways of saying that though you may broach your work without interest and without enthusiasm, you are gradually or suddenly seized by an interest, which up to a certain point continues to mount. With the genius this interest is greater than with the common man. As psychologists have pointed out, a man is not a genius because he concentrates more than the ordinary man; he concentrates more because he is a genius. His ideas overflow; they come with such rapidity, they change the aspects of his subject with such kaleidoscopic variety, they throw so many new and interesting and dazzling lights on it, that his attention is sustained by following them. The dullard, no matter how much of a plugger he may be, finds the utmost difficulty in sticking to any train of thought of his own, because his mind will produce only hackneyed and barren ideas, hardly worth attending to.

The problem, then in all creative work, is to seek to sustain the interest at the highest pitch, never allowing it to flag. As long as the interest is intense enough, physical and mental fatigue will not greatly matter. Eight times out of nine it is flagging interest, rather than real fatigue, which makes us quit. The phenomenon might be represented on a chart by two lines or curves, such as the political economists use for "demand curves" and supply curves." Starting at the top, and slanting downward (or starting low, mounting higher, and then curving down again), would be a curve or an irregular up and down line representing interest. Starting at the bottom and slanting upward, would be a curve or irregular line representing fatigue. At some point these two lines would meet; and that would be the point at which you would ordinarily quit.

There are two ways to put off this point. If by diversification, by turning from one subject to another, by changing the aspects considered even of a single subject; you can sustain or increase your interest, then the top line representing interest will not go down to meet the line representing fatigue; the fatigue line will have further to go, higher to mount; the point of intersection may be surprisingly postponed.

But if the two lines do meet, you have still a recourse, if you care to use it. That is your will. You can fight through the point by sheer effort, trusting that after a time either the upper interest line will rise again or the lower fatigue line will fall, allowing you another spell of achievement; and so on through other points of intersection. "Heroism," said W.T. Grenfell, "is endurance for one moment more."

I shall be told that this is a very dangerous doctrine, that if put into practice it would lead to overwork, overstrain and nervous breakdown. It is possible to overdo it; but I am convinced that for the overwhelming majority of those who read this, there is not the slightest danger of such a thing happening. Most breakdowns attributed to overwork do not come from overwork, but from worry, dissipation and unhygienic living. Indolence will always find excuses for its own existence; and the greatest of these has always been, and will always be, this bogey of "overwork."

XVI
MORAL COURAGE

I MUST extend a few warnings before we part, and I can do it briefly.

Never boast to your friends about your will-power. They are apt to become cynical and facetious, especially when you have broken some major or minor resolution in a fit of absent-mindedness. You want your friends to know of your will-power, but the best way for them to discover it will be through your actions, not your words.

Don't (O Don't), be a prig. A prig is person who has become vastly well satisfied with himself. His chief pastime is to fill the air with lamentations over the shortcomings of other people. He is satisfied with himself because he is so easily satisfied. He is the little Jack Horner who says, "What a good boy am I!" A prig's mind dwells on his successes and on what he has accomplished. Now true willpower is perfectly compatible with true humility, and a man of true humility dwells on his shortcomings and on what he has failed to accomplish. The prig is satisfied with himself because in his own eye he is realizing his ideals; but one of the reasons for this is simply that his ideals are low enough to make it easy to realize them. A man of true humility puts his ideal always a little beyond his reach. A prig for instance takes credit to himself because he reads good books. The man who is destined to grow criticizes himself because, though he reads good books, he does not think enough for himself. A prig admires himself because he has given $5 to the Red Cross. A true man, in the same financial circumstances, may be a little ashamed of himself because he has only given $15.

Things of a similar tenor have been said before. "It is in general more profitable," says Carlyle, "to reckon up our defects than to boast of our attainments." And the words of Phillips Brooks are more thrilling:

> Sad is the day for any man when he becomes absolutely satisfied with the life that he is living, the thoughts that he is thinking and the deeds that he is doing; when there ceases to be forever beating at the doors of his soul a desire to do something larger, which he feels and knows he was meant and intended to do.

To resume our admonitions. Don't try to be a "dominating personality" by shouting down your opponents or co-workers. Willpower has no necessary connection with noise.

Don't be stubborn. Especially don't be stubborn in your social recreations, under the impression that that is willpower. Don't say, "We will play bridge," whether anybody else wants to or not. Don't "break up the party" just because it won't play your way. Don't fancy that will-power is incompatible with making yourself agreeable.

The difference between stubbornness and backbone you may imagine to be merely a difference in invective. A man who stands for principles in which you believe, has backbone; a man who stands for principles in which you do not believe, is stubborn. But the true difference, as I conceive it, is that the stubborn man will not listen to reason. He will persist in a course he has adopted simply to maintain his vanity. He won't admit that he has been wrong, though, he may know it in his heart. His notion of will-power is sadly false. Will-power is consentaneous to the utmost spirit of conciliation. This does not mean compromise. The man with backbone is willing to listen to argument; he will keep his mind open. But he will not deviate an inch in principle if he knows himself to be right. He will give in before convincing argument; he is big enough to admit that he can make mistakes, and even that he has made one in this particular instance. But he will never give in because of mere lack of physical and moral courage.

And moral courage is the rarest of all the rare things of this earth. The war has shown that millions have physical courage. Millions were willing to face rifle and cannon, bombardment, poison gas, liquid fire, and the bayonet; to trust themselves to flying machines thousands of feet in air, under the fire of anti-aircraft guns and the machine guns of enemy planes; to go into submarines, perhaps to meet a horrible death. But how many had the courage merely to make themselves unpopular? The bitter truth must be told; that many enlisted or submitted to the draft on both sides of the conflict not because they were convinced that they were helping to save the world, not because they had any real hatred for the enemy, not to up-hold the right, but simply that they hadn't the moral courage to face the stigma of "slacker" or "conscientious objector."

Perhaps it would be unwise to take for granted that the passions of the war have completely cooled, and possibly many would miss the point if I were to discuss this question from the point of view of our own side. But let us look at it from the German side. The Germans surely had physical courage. Not all of them shouted "Kamerad," or if they did, it is rather strange that it took a world in arms more than four years to defeat them. But how many had moral courage in Germany? How many dared, like Maximilien Harden, to lift their voices against the dominant German creed, and how high dared he lift his? Fear of death? No; the soldiers faced death bravely. But they feared unpopularity. They dreaded the suspicion of their fellows.

What was needed in war is needed no less urgently in peace. How many persons in public or even in private life have the courage to say the thing that people do not like to hear? The ancient Greeks were not a superior race of people, but in the little city of Athens, in a period covering only a few hundred years, there came forth thinkers the splendor of whose fame has not been paralleled, certainly not exceeded, in all the nations of the world in all the thousand of years that have come since then. Where is the modern triumvirate of philosophers that is greater than Aristotle, Socrates and Plato? There may have been a number of reasons that brought this flowering of Greek culture, but one of them was this; that thought in Greece was free. A man could arrive at an opinion on a fundamental question different from that of his fellows without bringing himself into contempt. For a thousand years after Aristotle there were no thinkers; and the reason was, that thinking for oneself was despised. The authority of Aristotle was absolute. It applied not only to what he had positively said, but to what he had omitted to say. If it was not in Aristotle, it did not exist. When, in time, a few great spirits began to think for themselves, they faced a bitter struggle. Galileo, supporting the discovery of Copernicus that the earth revolved around the sun, and not the sun around the earth, was compelled publicly to repudiate it. Bacon had to plead against the authority of Aristotle. Locke had to write:

> some will not admit an opinion not authorized by men of old, who were then all giants in knowledge. Nothing is to be put into the treasury of truth or knowledge which has not the stamp of Greece or Rome upon it, and since their

days will scarce allow that men have been able to see, think or write.

What can it profit a man to be able to think, if he does not dare to? One must have the courage to go where the mind leads, no matter how startling the conclusion, how shattering, how much it may hurt oneself or a particular class, no matter how unfashionable or how obnoxious it may at first seem. This may require the courage to stand against the whole world. Great is the man who has that courage, for he indeed has achieved will-power.

THE END

Made in the USA
Lexington, KY
28 September 2017